BRIGHT NOTES

MOLL FLANDERS BY DANIEL DEFOE

Intelligent Education

Nashville, Tennessee

BRIGHT NOTES: Moll Flanders
www.BrightNotes.com

No part of this publication may be used or reproduced in any manner whatsoever without written permission, except in the case of brief quotations in critical articles and reviews. For permissions, contact Influence Publishers http://www.influencepublishers.com.

ISBN: 978-1-645420-70-5 (Paperback)
ISBN: 978-1-645420-71-2 (eBook)

Published in accordance with the U.S. Copyright Office Orphan Works and Mass Digitization report of the register of copyrights, June 2015.

Originally published by Monarch Press.
David A. Gooding, 1965
2019 Edition published by Influence Publishers.

Interior design by Lapiz Digital Services. Cover Design by Thinkpen Designs.

Printed in the United States of America.

Library of Congress Cataloging-in-Publication Data forthcoming.
Names: Intelligent Education
Title: BRIGHT NOTES: Moll Flanders
Subject: STU004000 STUDY AIDS / Book Notes

CONTENTS

1)	Introduction to Daniel Defoe	1
2)	Textual Analysis	
	Part I: The Amorous Adventures of Moll Flanders	14
	Part II: The Disreputable Deeds of Moll Flanders	67
3)	Character Analyses	107
4)	Critical Commentary	121
5)	Essay Questions and Answers	132
6)	Glossary of Terms	144
7)	Bibliography	148

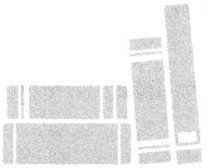

INTRODUCTION TO DANIEL DEFOE

INTRODUCTION

Daniel Defoe is best known as the author of *Robinson Crusoe*. However, his life encompassed such a diversity of activities that no single word such as "novelist" adequately describes him. His literary output was enormous, with some five hundred publications to his credit, but the few works of fiction were written late in his life. Propagandist and pamphleteer, novelist and reporter, Defoe also found time to write histories, biographies, travelogues and poetry. In addition to his literary activities, Defoe also pursued a number of other careers. He prided himself on his business ability and always maintained that he was primarily a merchant. For a number of years he also acted as a secret agent for Robert Harley, the Secretary of State. Very much involved with contemporary affairs, Defoe's writings, whether fictional, reportorial or polemical, reflect the interests and opinions of his times. For a fuller understanding of Defoe himself, it is therefore necessary to know something about his England.

HISTORICAL BACKGROUND: THE MONARCHS

During Defoe's lifetime (1660–1731), six monarchs reigned in England. The Stuart king, Charles II, was restored to the throne which had been vacant since his father's beheading twelve years before, in 1660. Charles II had considerably more tact than his ancestors and did not allow his personal preference for absolute rule and Roman Catholicism to offend the more democratic and Protestant susceptibilities of his subjects. His brother James II, who succeeded him in 1685, was less wise and openly avowed his Roman Catholicism. As a direct result of the birth of a son in 1688, the "Glorious Revolution" (so-called because it was brief and bloodless), replaced James by his elder, Protestant daughter, Mary and her husband William of Orange. They had no children and were succeeded by Mary's younger sister Anne in 1702. None of Anne's children survived her, so she was succeeded by a distant, Protestant relation, George I of Hanover, in 1714. His son, George II, ascended the throne in 1727.

HISTORICAL BACKGROUND: WAR WITH FRANCE

While Charles II and James II reigned, England maintained peaceful relations with Louis XIV's France. However, William III soon involved England in his life long feud with the French. Although peace was declared in 1697, war again broke out in 1701. This, the "war of the Spanish succession," continued until 1713. In both cases England was the victor.

HISTORICAL BACKGROUND: POLITICAL

The terms of the settlement by which William and Mary ascended the throne vacated by James II established that

England would be a constitutional monarchy, governed by Parliament. Although the king remained in nominal control, his ministers now had more power than previously. The ministers were members of Parliament and they retained office only as long as they were able to control Parliament. Since no one man could be sure of the support of more than a few of the members of the House of Commons, several men who had similar ideas concerning the way in which the country should be run would join together. In this way political parties were formed. During Defoe's life time there were two parties, called the Whigs and the Tories. The Tories belonged to the upper classes, supported the supremacy of the Church of England and favored the restoration of the Stuart monarchy in the person of James II's son, the "Old Pretender." The Whigs, on the other hand, often belonged to the middle class, favored toleration for the various Protestant groups and supported the Hanoverian dynasty. Between the two extremes there were many moderates. All those Protestants who did not belong to the Church of England (also known as the Anglican Church) were called Dissenters. Dissenters were not permitted to hold office, but many of them did by attending the Anglican Church occasionally. Defoe was against this practice of "occasional conformity" and wrote a pamphlet attacking it.

HISTORICAL BACKGROUND: SCOTLAND

During the period of the Stuart monarchs, Scotland and England were allied because they shared the same king. James I of England was also James VI of Scotland. With the overthrow of the Stuart dynasty in 1688, it became apparent that closer political ties with Scotland would have to be established. Therefore, the two countries were legally unified by the Act of Union in 1707. Defoe was quite active in furthering this treaty which brought England and Scotland together.

HISTORICAL BACKGROUND: TRADE AND THE MIDDLE CLASS

The seventeenth and eighteenth centuries witnessed the rise of the middle class to a position of power and prestige. Their influence would cause England, in the nineteenth century, to be known as a "nation of shopkeepers." Trade was occupying a more important position in the nation's economy than it ever had before. With ability, luck and a few influential friends, a young man could rise to be a great merchant. He might even marry the daughter of a duke or become a member of the nobility himself. Daniel Defoe undoubtedly had ambitions of this nature.

DEFOE'S CHILDHOOD

Born sometime in 1660 (the year of Charles II's restoration to the throne), Defoe was the son of a Dissenting tradesman. His father, James Foe, did not believe in infant baptism, so we have no record of Defoe's birth. (Defoe added the aristocratic prefix "De" to his family name toward the end of the century.) Born and brought up in London. Defoe spent the greater part of his life in or near it. He was probably only five years old when the great plague of 1665–66 broke out, but he remembered what he was told about the tragic epidemic and wrote the effective Journal of the Plague Year in 1722. In September of 1666 occurred the great fire of London which destroyed most of the old city, but stopped short a few blocks from the Foe home. Defoe went to schools run by the Dissenters, and the education he acquired here stressed subjects such as history and geography, rather than the Latin and Greek which predominated at the universities of Oxford and Cambridge (which were open only to Anglicans). He originally intended to study for the Presbyterian ministry, but decided that he was unsuitable and instead prepared himself to become a merchant, like his father.

THE YOUNG MERCHANT

By 1683, Defoe was established as a merchant, dealing primarily in haberdashery. The following year, he married Mary Tuffley, whose father was moderately wealthy. Although in later years Defoe was able to give sound advice to young men beginning business careers, he never followed his own precepts. He persistently overreached himself in financial matters, becoming involved in more risky and ultimately unsuccessful ventures than profitable undertakings. He was also involved in a number of law suits. Biographers differ on how guilty he was of the many charges of dishonesty leveled against him, but it is unlikely that he was completely innocent in all cases. Defoe also suffered some severe financial losses as a direct result of King William's war with the French, when ships he insured were captured by the enemy. As a result of bad luck, poor judgment and perhaps dishonesty, Defoe found himself unable to pay his bills and was declared a bankrupt in 1692. Within ten years, the greater part of the debt had been repaid, but Defoe was forever after haunted by the threat of debtors' prison.

POLITICAL ASSOCIATIONS

Defoe, as a good Dissenter, feared the consequences of a Roman Catholic sovereign. He therefore supported the uprising of 1685 (which attempted to replace James II by Charles II's natural son, the Protestant Duke of Monmouth) but escaped punishment when the revolt failed. Defoe was firmer in his support of

William III; one of his first political pamphlets, *A Letter to a Dissenter* from his friend at the Hague (published anonymously in the summer of 1688), openly criticized James II's policies. Welcoming William III's arrival in England, Defoe soon made himself useful to the new monarch and his ministers, and was rewarded by several minor government positions. By the end of the century, Defoe was writing pamphlets fairly regularly in support of William's policies. In 1701, Defoe published a satirical poem, *The True-Born Englishman*, as an answer to critics who complained that England was being overrun by "foreigners" that is, by William III's Dutch friends and advisers. The point of the extremely popular poem was that the ancestor of all Englishmen were foreigners once. During the same year, Defoe did an even greater service for William in writing *Legion's Memorial* to the House of Commons, Parliament, instead of voting military supplies to support William's war, had been bickering about unimportant matters. Defoe's pamphlet, which he personally gave to Robert Harley, then Speaker of the House, warned Commons that Parliament should serve the people, and if it did not, the people could overthrow it.

FALL FROM FAVOR

Defoe felt that his position was now secure. Unfortunately, William III died on March 8, 1702. His sister-in-law, Anne, favored the extreme Tories, so Defoe, as a Dissenting Whig could hope for no more royal favors. At the end of this year, angered by sermons and speeches advocating religious persecution of all Dissenting sects, Defoe anonymously published a pamphlet called *The Shortest Way with the Dissenters*. Written tongue-in-cheek, *The Shortest Way* advocated extreme repressive measures against the Dissenters, such as hanging and banishment. Unfortunately, the sermons Defoe was satirizing used language that was just as violent, and for a while everyone thought that the anonymous author was sincere. When it was found that Defoe was the author, both the Dissenters and the Tories were extremely angry with him and the Tories decided that he should be punished. Accordingly, Defoe was charged with writing a seditious libel and sentenced to the extremely severe punishment of standing three times in the pillory, paying a fine, and remaining in prison for an indefinite time. Defoe's Whig friends managed affairs so that, while Defoe had to stand in the pillory (a T-shaped construction with holes for the head and hands) his public exposure turned into a personal triumph. Instead of jeering and throwing things at him, the crowd cheered and bought copies of his latest **satire**, *A Hymn to the Pillory*. The calculating Harley, having decided that Defoe's pen would be useful, waited several months to insure Defoe's gratitude and then arranged his release from prison. Defoe was now a hero to the London mob and was secretly bound to the ambitious Harley.

SECRET AGENT DEFOE

Robert Harley (later created Earl of Oxford) became Secretary of State in 1704. He was a moderate Tory, but Defoe seemed to have no trouble in adapting his political beliefs to conform with Harley's. There was, basically, little difference between the moderate Whig and Tory positions. Defoe's duties, as Harley's protege, consisted of writing pamphlets and newspaper articles in support of government policy, taking informal public opinion polls throughout England and "campaigning" for the election of Harley's supporters. His usefulness could last only as long as his connection with Harley remained a secret. Defoe remained a servant of the Ministry, through several different administrations, until the death of Queen Anne in 1714.

EDITOR AND JOURNALIST

While Defoe was traveling around England and Scotland on Harley's behalf, he was also occupied by his duties as editor of *A Weekly Review of the Affairs of France*. The name soon proved undescriptive of the contents, for in the *Review* (which came out thrice weekly) Defoe discussed a variety of timely subjects. (*The Review* and a number of publications like it were the eighteenth-century equivalent of *Time* and *Newsweek* although they gave more space to editorials than to actual news.) At the same time he published numerous pamphlets and treatises giving his views on such things as economics, public morality and the great storm of 1703. Defoe's account of the great storm represents the beginning of his career as a reporter. He investigated the effects of the storm himself, and secured descriptions of it from many people who witnessed it. He also reported on such strange matters as the alleged disappearance of an island in the West Indies and a ghostly visitation which he called *The Apparition of Mrs. Veal*.

UNOFFICIAL GOVERNMENT CENSOR

After Queen Anne's death in 1714, Defoe was without government employment for a time until George I's Whig Cabinet decided to make use of his talents. By this time, Defoe's association with the moderate Tory Harley was well known, and it was thought that Defoe was himself a Tory. It was therefore easy for him to obtain a position as editor of a Tory newspaper.

What was not known was that he was in the employ of the Whigs and that his purpose was to soften the Tory attacks on the Government. Defoe's principal association was with the *Weekly Journal* published by Nathaniel Mist. Defoe served as an unofficial government censor on extreme Tory periodicals for several years, acting so circumspectly that no one suspected his connection with the Whig ministry.

FAMILY LIFE

Defoe's marriage to Mary Tuffley appears to have been reasonably happy. They had two sons and six daughters, but two of the daughters died young. Some biographers have asserted that Defoe also had an illegitimate son, but John Robert Moore, in his biography, *Daniel Defoe: Citizen of the Modern World*, denies this, One of Defoe's sons, Benjamin, became a journalist, but lacked his father's ability. Defoe's youngest daughter, Sophia, was his favorite. There are hints in Defoe's letters and moralistic treatises that his sons, particularly Daniel, Jr., were ungrateful and lacking in respect for their father.

ECONOMIST

Defoe was extremely interested in economics. *The Review* devoted more space to this subject than to any other. One of his most popular works was *The Complete English Tradesman* (1725) in which he gave sound advice, most of it based on his own business failures. His first book, *Essay on Projects* (1698) contained many excellent suggestions for improving the English economy, such as an income tax, more lenient treatment of bankrupts and improvements in the banking system.

BRIGHT NOTES STUDY GUIDE

ROBINSON CRUSOE

By 1719, Defoe's political career was coming to an end. However, in the remaining twelve years of his life, Defoe published a great many works, including all of his novels, several historical and biographical works and his famous *A Tour thro' the whole Island of Great Britain*. It is remarkable that the bulk of his literary compositions was written when he was past fifty. *Robinson Crusoe*, published in 1719, was immensely popular during his lifetime. It was based on the adventures of a man named Alexander Selkirk, who lived alone for four years on an island, and purported to be autobiographical, rather than fictional. *Robinson Crusoe* was so successful that Defoe brought out two further volumes, *Further Adventures of Robinson Crusoe*, and *Serious Reflections of Robinson Crusoe*, neither of which is much remembered today.

MOLL FLANDERS: BACKGROUND

A popular literary form at this was time the criminal life, or rogue biography. Condemned criminals would give their stories to someone for publication. Enterprising journalist, among them Defoe, frequently paid the condemned man to hand them the manuscript (previously written by the journalists himself) at the gallows, thus gaining considerable free publicity. Since the lives of most of these unfortunates were not terribly interesting, most of the biographies contained more fiction than fact. *Moll Flanders* was written in this tradition and, like *Robinson Crusoe*, was supposed to be the autobiography of a real person. Although the novel is supposed to have been written in 1683, Defoe published it (and probably wrote it) in 1722. In *Moll Flanders*, Defoe describes England, and especially London, as it was in the early eighteenth century.

MOLL FLANDERS: PLOT

The full title of *Moll Flanders* gives an excellent description of the contents: "The Fortunes. and Misfortunes of the Famous Moll Flanders, who was born in Newgate, and during a Life of continued Variety, for Threescore Years, besides her Childhood, was Twelve Year a Whore, five times a Wife (whereof once to her own Brother), Twelve Year a Thief, Eight Year a Transported Felon in Virginia, at last grew Rich, lived Honest, and died a Penitent, Written from her own Memorandums ..." The title is obviously designed to attract those who want to mix sensational reading with moral uplift. Moll's mother, convicted of stealing a small amount of cloth, was saved from the gallows only because of her pregnancy. By strange turns of fortune, Moll spends her 'teens with a moderately wealthy family. She becomes the mistress of the elder brother and then marries the younger brother. When her husband dies she marries a spendthrift and when he flees the country to avoid debtor's prison, marries once more, this time to a wealthy American. To her dismay, she finds after several years that her American husband is also her half-brother. Returning to England, Moll becomes mistress to a married man. When he leaves her, Moll marries for the fourth time. Her new husband, Jemmy, soon reveals that he is penniless and that he has married her only because he thought she was wealthy. They part affectionately agreeing that each is free to remarry. Moll soon marries for the fifth time and when, after some years, she is left a widow, she enters on a life of crime. Nearly half the book recounts Moll's profitable, though illegal career, but finally she is caught, taken to Newgate prison and sentenced to death. Her plea that her sentence be commuted to transportation to the colonies is granted and, having discovered that Jemmy is awaiting trial as a highwayman, she convinces him to go with her. Arriving in Virginia, Moll and Jemmy buy their freedom and begin a new life as planters. The novel ends with Moll's declaration that she and

Jemmy, who are now elderly and wealthy, intend to spend the remainder of their lives in sincere repentance.

MOLL FLANDERS: PURPOSE

Defoe makes it quite clear, in his preface to *Moll Flanders*, that there is a moral to the story. Molls "fortunes and misfortunes" illustrate the maxim that "crime does not pay." Throughout the novel, Moll reprimands herself for her evil life and laments that her poverty compels her to embrace a life of crime. Defoe also manages to insert several of his schemes for the prevention of crime. For instance, he has Moll suggest that the government care for the children of criminals, training them to be useful individuals. While, toward the end of her life, Moll repents of the evil she has done, we note that she does not do so until she is financially secure and quite elderly. Some critics maintain that Defoe merely inserted moral comments to justify an otherwise sensational story. However, difficult though it is to believe, it appears that Defoe really thought that the lurid details of *Moll Flanders* would serve as a warning and encourage readers to amend their lives.

DEFOE'S OTHER NOVELS

Most of Defoe's novels are of the same **genre** as *Moll Flanders*, the rogue biography. Colonel Jack, which appeared toward the end of 1722, involved the hero in both crime and political rebellion. However, Colonel Jack repents (before old age sets in), becoming a highly respectable gentleman. The story of another rebel is recounted in *The Memoirs of a Cavalier* (1720). In the same year appeared Captain Singleton, which combines the current interest in far-off places (half the book is set in

Madagascar) with the rogue biography. Another of Defoe's more famous novels is *Roxana,* published in 1724. Roxana is a lady of pleasure who seems to have no moral sense at all. However, in the end she too repents. All of Defoe's novels, including *Robinson Crusoe,* have highly righteous endings, This was due partly to Defoe's own religious training and to the prevailing temper of the times: it did not matter what the character did, so long as he was sorry afterwards.

DEFOE'S LAST YEARS

During most of his life, Defoe lived in the fear of debtors' prison. Although he had paid most of his debts by 1702, he knew that a creditor could demand full payment at any time. Defoe's political enemies sometimes arranged to have debts which had already been paid, or which had never been contracted, brought up for payment. In those days, there was little legal protection for a former bankrupt. During much of his career, Defoe had powerful friends who could keep him out of prison, but toward the end of his life he had no such protection. He took the precaution of transferring all of his property to his son Daniel, so that creditors would be unable to lay claims to it. In the last year of his life, Defoe went into hiding, probably to escape one of these creditors. He was so afraid of being found that he would not permit his family to visit him openly. Finally, on April 24, 1731, he died "of a lethargy" (probably meaning old age). After such a long and vigorous life, it seems anti-climactic that he should die, alone, and in furnished rooms. Two days later he was buried in obscurity, but even those journals politically opposed to him honored him in their obituaries.

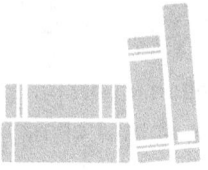

MOLL FLANDERS

TEXTUAL ANALYSIS

PART I: THE AMOROUS ADVENTURES OF MOLL FLANDERS

AUTHOR'S PREFACE

Defoe comments that there are so many novels and romances being published that the concealment of Moll's true name will probably prevent many people from believing that her story is true

Comment

The novels and romances which Defoe talks about were not novels in the sense that we use the term. The novel as a literary form did not come into being until the appearance of Richardson's *Pamela* in 1740. This subject will be dealt with more fully in the Critical Commentary section

Defoe admits that he has rewritten Moll's "memoirs" primarily because the language she uses is unsuitable. He casts some doubt on the depth of Moll's "repentance," but indicates that he has edited her manuscript in such a way that one cannot help but be the instructed by it. After citing several examples of the high moral tone of the work, Defoe notes that all the evil characters either come to a bad end or repent. Because of the lessons contained in the book, by which the reader can learn both how to avoid falling into evil ways and how to prevent being victimized by evil-doers, Defoe feels justified in recommending the work. The preface ends with a comment that the lives of Moll's governess and of her husband Jemmy may yet be published.

Comment

Defoe never wrote the novels which he hints at, although he undoubtedly intended to if *Moll Flanders* were sufficiently popular.

CHAPTER I: CHILDHOOD

[Editor's Note: *Moll Flanders* has no subdivisions. The divisions into two parts and 14 chapters, and the titles of the parts and chapters, has been made for the sake of convenience.] The novel opens with Moll's declaration that she cannot reveal her true name because of the danger of being arrested for past crimes. Noting that in one country the Government takes care of the children of criminals, teaching them a useful and honest trade, Moll theorizes that if this had been the case in England, she would not have been tempted into evil ways.

Comment

While Moll's idea for preserving the virtue of these unfortunate children is a good one, we cannot feel that she is justified in using her own early circumstances as an excuse for her later life. As we shall see, she was raised by respectable individuals and was taught needlework at an early age. If she had wanted to, she could have supported herself (although she would have been far from wealthy) by honest means. But then there would have been no story!

Moll now begins the story of her life. Her mother, having been convicted of a small theft, was sentenced to be hanged. Punishment was deferred until after her child had been born and then the sentence was commuted to transportation to the Colonies.

Comment

During the eighteenth century, most crimes having to do with property were punishable by death. This did not act as a deterrent however, for if one could be hanged for stealing a handkerchief, one might as well steal the contents of a shop and kill the owner at the same time. The expression, "I might as well be hanged for a sheep as a lamb" comes from this period and was literally true. For the criminal, the prison was merely a place in which to await trial and punishment. Only in the case of someone convicted of a crime against the state (for instance seditious libel, of which Defoe was found guilty) was the sentence a prison term. As a result of the harsh laws, death sentences were frequently commuted to "transportation" for varying periods of time, depending on the nature of the original offense. The criminal was "transported" to the plantations, usually Virginia or Carolina, where he was hired by a planter and became a bond-servant. The contract could not be broken by the felon. After he had completed his term, he was free to go back to England, but he generally did not have the money to pay for passage and stayed in the colonies. After the American Revolution, convicts were frequently transported to Australia.

Moll knows little about her infancy, but she does remember that she fell in with a group of gypsies. She tells us that the gypsies left her (or she ran away, she does not know which) at Colchester and because of her youth (she was about three years old) the parish officers pitied and took care of her.

Comment

Until the nineteenth century, England followed the sixteenth-century Poor Law. Each community (or parish) provided for those of its citizens who were unable to support themselves. Since the cost was divided among the taxpayers, who naturally were against high taxes, the town officials tried to prevent anyone likely to become unemployed from settling there. Efforts were made to return the poor person and his family to the place of his birth, or of his longest residence. Parish officers were particularly wary of orphans who, of course, would be unable to support themselves for quite a long time.

Moll is placed with a woman who runs a small school in her home and is quite happy until, at the age of eight, she learns that she is to become a domestic servant. This upsets her greatly for as she tells her foster mother, she wants to become a gentlewoman. She asserts that she will be able to earn her living by sewing. Moll's foster mother tells the Mayor about her charge's ambition and he, in turn, tells his wife and daughters. They are highly amused and come to visit Moll, asking her how she defines "gentlewoman." Moll explains that a gentlewoman is one who is not a domestic servant, but earns her own living. Later she points out to her nurse (as she calls her foster mother) someone whom she calls a "gentlewoman." The nurse is somewhat disturbed, because the woman to whom Moll refers has had several illegitimate children, but Moll does not understand this and insists that she will be that kind of gentlewoman.

Comment

Here we see an ironic prophecy, for Moll fulfills her childish ambition with a vengeance.

Moll becomes quite popular with the ladies of the town and they frequently give her small amounts of money and sewing to do. Finally one of the ladies invites Moll to visit for a week. This experience spoils Moll a little, giving her a taste for greater luxury, but she returns to her nurse's home. About a year later, when Moll is fourteen, her nurse dies.

Comment

Moll is not upset at the old woman's death so much as at the difficult circumstances in which she finds herself. She is so frightened at being alone without any material security, that as she tells us, she is even willing to become a servant.

Fortunately for Moll, the lady with whom she stayed the year before hears of her misfortune and takes her into her own home. Here Moll is raised with the daughters of the house, learning all the accomplishments of a well-brought-up young lady such as dancing, French and music. She notes that she learned very quickly and was also much better-looking than the daughters of the house.

CHAPTER 2: COURTSHIP AND FIRST MARRIAGE

Until now, Moll tells us, she has had unusual advantages and has never strayed from the path of virtue. Now she begins the story of her undoing. The lady with whom she lives has, besides her daughters, two sons, the elder of whom determines to make Moll his mistress. He compliments her extravagantly, both to her face and when she is absent (although he makes sure that she overhears his favorable remarks). One of the sisters takes exception to the flattering words of the Elder Brother and says that no matter how beautiful and accomplished a woman is, no man will marry her if she does not have money. At this, the Younger Brother asserts that money does not matter and that he certainly will not marry solely for money.

Comment

Defoe names very few of the characters in *Moll Flanders*. Thus the Elder Brother, who plays such an important part in the novel, is given no name, while the Younger Brother is known only as Robert or Robin. We are not told even his name until much later in the story. Moll's first name is apparently Elizabeth or Betty, for she is called "Mrs. Betty." "Mrs." is short for Mistress and was a polite form of address applied to women whether married or not.

Robin's statement leads to an argument during which the Elder Brother implies that his sister has money but nothing else in her favor and is still unable to find a husband. Robin also joins in, infuriating the sister by hinting that "Mrs. Betty" may make a better marriage, and sooner, than the sister.

Some days later the Elder Brother comes upon Moll when she is alone. He seizes the opportunity to kiss her and proclaim his love for her. Moll comments that the Elder Brother's praise of her and declaration of his love for her increased her vanity which prevented her from analyzing his motives. Soon after this the Elder Brother again arranges to see Moll alone. Kissing her passionately, he vows he loves her and declares that he will marry her as soon as he comes into his inheritance (that is, when his father dies). Upon leaving her, he gives her five guineas.

Comment

Five guineas represented a large sum of money. A guinea was worth twenty-one shillings; a pound equaled twenty shillings and a shilling represented twelve pence. In 1696, it was calculated that the average agricultural laborer earned a shilling a day. Thus it can be seen that the eighteenth-century pound had great value. In fact, many people lived quite comfortably on an income of fifty pounds a year.

Moll notes that had the Elder Brother known how little she valued her virtue, he would not have expended so much effort on making her his mistress. She adds that if she had acted properly, she would have insisted that he either marry her at once or give her regular and complete financial support.

At last the Elder Brother completes his seduction of Moll. Asking her, in front of his sisters, to run several errands for him, he catches up with her some distance from home and takes her to a house which he has borrowed for the occasion. After promising to marry her as soon as his father dies, and to give her a hundred guineas a year until that time, he gains his end. Moll tells us that their illicit relationship continued for about six months without anyone suspecting them.

The Colchester family grows decidedly cool towards Moll, not because of her relationship with the Elder Brother, of which they are completely unaware, but because of the marked attention paid her by Robin. He tells Moll that he loves her and asks her to marry him, saying that his earnings as a lawyer will support them comfortably. His intentions seem to be completely honorable. Moll is quite disturbed; she feels that she cannot accept his proposal of marriage because of her liaison with his brother. She also wonders why her lover has not mentioned marriage to her since she became his mistress.

Comment

At that time, having sexual relations with two brothers (or two sisters) was considered incestuous.

Finally, since there is talk in the family of dismissing Moll, she decides to ask the Elder Brother for advice. She does not mention Robin's proposal but says that she is afraid the family has discovered their affair. He calms her "fears" and tells her that his family is angry because Robin has made no secret of his love for her. The Moll explains the true cause of her concern: once it is known that she has refused Robin's proposal the family will demand to know the reason and then her liaison with the elder Brother will become known. The Elder Brother surprises her greatly by telling her not to give Robin a definite answer yet, thus hinting that he may suggest that she accept his brother's proposal. He then leaves her, promising to talk to his brother and then discuss the matter further with her.

After about a week, the two brothers finally discuss the younger one's attachment to Moll. The latter states that he loves her, wants to marry her and is certain she will accept him. The Elder Brother relates the entire conversation to Moll, who reiterates her determination to refuse Robin. However, the Elder Brother advises her to accept. Pointing out that his father shows no signs of dying for many years, he says that if he were to marry her now, he would undoubtedly be disinherited. Moll is naturally quite angry at this and reminds him that he has always maintained she is his wife in fact, if not in law. Now she feels that he never intended to marry her. Crying that she loves him, she says she would rather be his mistress than his brother's wife.

Moll and the Elder Brother have several interviews of this nature until finally the Elder Brother tells her quite bluntly that the only solution to the problem is to accept Robin's proposal. At this Moll puts up a great fuss. The Elder Brother states that he will keep his promise to support her but will no longer treat her as his mistress because she may become his sister-in-law. Moll tells us that this upsets her even more, because she loves him and has long dreamed of becoming his wife.

| Comment

Characteristically, Moll describes her love for the Elder Brother and her mercenary ambitions in the same sentence. It was customary at this time for the eldest son to inherit the whole estate. Thus the Elder Brother will eventually be much richer and have a higher social position than Robin, the younger son.

Moll is so upset by the Elder Brother's advice that she becomes quite ill. The illness lasts for about five weeks and her convalescence is very slow. The doctors tell the family that Moll must be in love, or she would make a more rapid recovery. The entire family begins questioning her but she steadfastly maintains that she is not in love. Robin declares that he wishes she loved him because he would be glad to marry her.

| Comment

We learn here for the first time that the Younger Brother is called Robin, or Robert. We never do find out the names of any of the other members of the family.

He adds that he has spoken to "Mrs. Betty" on several occasions, but cannot convince her that he is serious. His mother talks to Moll, who assures her that there is nothing between her and Robin, and that she has always thought him to be joking when he talked of love. Robin's sisters express their conviction that Moll is quite anxious to marry him and make a number of uncomplimentary remarks. Their ill-humor is deepened by jealousy, for both Robin and the Elder Brother continually point out that the girls have no suitors and that Moll, though poor, is much prettier than they are.

| Comment

For a repentant old lady of seventy, Moll certainly enjoys relating the compliments she says were bestowed on her when she was young. We have the feeling that she has always enjoyed herself enormously and now, in her old age, derives considerable satisfaction from remembering what a talented, beautiful woman she once was.

Robin, however, insists that he does not know whether Moll will accept him and adds that she may love someone else. The sisters comment that this is impossible, for she does not know anyone. Robin asks his brother whether he is the object of Moll's affection. The Elder Brother is naturally greatly upset, thinking that his brother suspects him, but answers that he has nothing to do with women like Moll.

Worried by Robin's comment, the Elder Brother decides to ask Moll about it. He has not seen her since she became ill. Asking his sister if he may see Moll, he makes a great joke of the visit, constantly teasing her about the rumor that she is in love. Finally he gets his sister out of the room by asking her to fetch his flute, and at once asks Moll if anyone knows of their relationship. She reassures him and then declares that it is her love for him which has retarded her recovery. She vows that she will never marry Robin and says that she will leave Colchester as soon as she is well.

Moll tells us that during the next four months she recovers slowly from her illness, but continues to be quite depressed. Knowing that there is talk of asking her to leave once she is well, she finally talks to the lady of the house about it. The subject of Robin naturally comes up and Moll states that although he has proposed marriage to her on several occasions, she has always refused him because she knows his parents would be against it. She says that she has told Robin that she will marry him only if his parents consent to it.

The lady of the house is naturally very surprised at Moll's unusually honorable behavior and compliments her on her excellent sense. Arranging to talk to Robin before Moll has a chance to see him, she finds that he gives the same account as Moll. Finding Moll's story confirmed, both the lady of the house and her daughters change their opinion about the girl's motives. Robin assures the women that he really does want to marry Moll and begs his mother for her consent to the match.

The Elder Brother is asked for advice and much to Moll's dismay, sides with Robin. His mother asks him to talk to Moll, to find out if she really will marry robin only with his parents' consent. After kissing her, the Elder Brother immediately begins trying to talk Moll into marrying Robin. He declares that he will always love her, but will henceforth treat her as a sister, whether she marries Robin or not. Pointing out the advantages of a marriage to Robin, the Elder Brother is careful to emphasize the difficulties and dangers of the unmarried woman who has lost her virtue.

Comment

During the eighteenth century a woman's position in society was entirely dependent on her husband's or father's. The unmarried woman found herself in an extremely difficult situation, for the only employment open to her was in domestic service, needlework or the care of children. The few women who exercised some independence (such as Fanny Burney, the author of *Evalina*) had the legal protection of a male relative. Since Moll has no relatives, her only path to financial security and social position lies through marriage. If she does not marry, and it becomes known that she has lost her virtue, she will be able to support herself only by being a prostitute.

Finally the Elder Brother persuades Moll to consent to the marriage.

After this, the Elder Brother also induces his mother to permit the marriage. The father of the family, who is away, is informed of the affair by letter and Robin and Moll are at last married.

Comment

The father of the family, Defoe caustically informs us, is too taken up with business to have time for his children. If he had acted as a proper father, the author implies, this situation would never have arisen. It is just such situations as this that Defoe covered in his book of domestic advice, *The Family Instructor*.

We are told that the Elder Brother performs one more useful service by getting Robin very drunk after the wedding so that he does not suspect Moll is not a virgin.

Moll summarizes the events of the next five years in a short paragraph. She confesses that although Robin was an excellent husband, she never loved him and always wished for his brother.

Comment

According to the strict Puritan code, Moll is guilty of incest because she has desired it. In Puritan eyes the intention is as bad as the deed.

They have two children and at the end of five years Robin dies, leaving Moll very little money. She leaves the children with their paternal grandparents and goes off to make her fortune with a capital of about twelve hundred pounds.

Comment

Moll seldom seems to have any maternal feelings. She tells us that she has two children by her first husband but she shows no hesitation in leaving them. She never tries to see them again and even when, years later, she happens to be in Colchester, she makes no inquiries concerning them. Her real concern is the amount of her fortune, which she knows to the penny.

CHAPTER 3: THE YOUNG WIDOW

Moll remains in London and is quite popular. However, she finds that most of the likeable men she meets have no desire to marry. She is determined not to make the same mistake she did with the Elder Brother and, since she has enough money to live on for a while, can afford to be choosy. Telling us that she would not mind being the wife of a prosperous tradesman, she adds that her husband must also look and act like a gentleman. At last Moll finds the gentleman-tradesman she has been looking for, but soon discovers that he is a terrible spendthrift. At this point in the narrative, Moll's repentant old age remarks that she was virtuous during this period in her life only because of her vanity and her money. Her more practical self comments that she would have been much better off financially becoming the mistress of her landlady's brother.

Comment

It is already apparent that Moll's moral standards are determined by the amount of money she commands. As she points out here, she believes no woman who has her own money should become someone's mistress. The implication is that only the rich can afford to be moral.

The gentleman-tradesman who becomes Moll's second husband is a draper by trade, but it is doubtful that his business was ever very successful. He is too much a gentleman and delights in appearing more wealthy than he really is. Moll's little fortune, and all of his own money, are quickly spent. As an example, Moll describes a vacation they took, going to Oxford in a coach with six servants and six horses. The trip was enjoyable, for they were treated as nobility and were undoubtedly charged at that rate. Moll tells us that they saw all the sights of Oxford and pretended that they were looking for tutors for a non-existent nephew. The cost of the twelve-day journey was about 93 pounds.

Comment

That amount, 93 pounds, was enough to keep middle-class people very comfortably for well over a year.

All this heavy expenditure causes their money to disappear quite rapidly. After a little more than two years, her husband is arrested for debt. Moll tells us that she knew this would happen and had been setting a little money aside. After his arrest, the gentleman-tradesman tells Moll to take all the valuables she can from the house and shop, because if she does not, his creditors will claim everything and she will be left destitute. He further tells her that he plans to escape and leave England. This he does very soon thereafter, nearly breaking his neck in the process, and Moll never sees him again. However, he does write to her from France to tell her about some cloth he had pawned. She redeems this, making a nice profit on it.

MOLL FLANDERS

Comment

Defoe was only too well aware of the laws and procedures governing bankruptcy. He himself went bankrupt at a fairly early age, and was hounded by creditors for the rest of his life.

Moll is now in a difficult position for she has, in money and possessions, only about five hundred pounds. What is worse from her point of view, she is still married, although she knows she will never see her husband again. She tells us, in a very off-hand manner, that the only child of her second marriage died. She is also afraid that her husband's creditors may find her, so she goes into the Mint, dressed as a widow and assuming the name of Mrs. Flanders.

Comment

In the eighteenth century, debtors could be put in prison until they paid their creditors. Many unfortunate men died in debtors' prison, since it was impossible for them to earn any money with which to pay off their debts. However, there were places where a debtor could be safe from his creditors. One of these was known as the Mint (because coins had been minted there in Tudor times). It was located in Southwark, the district across the river Thames from the City of London. The City had no legal jurisdiction over this area, so no debtor could be arrested as long as he remained in the Mint. The Mint, as a refuge for debtors, was abolished in 1723. There were other places where a debtor could take refuge. Defoe knew them all.

Moll finds that the company is not much to her liking for although she is very popular with the debtors, they all have dishonorable designs on her and show great weakness of character by spending what little money they have on immoral pastimes. She says that many of them, upbraiding themselves for their evil ways, will spend just a little more on a drink in honor of their long-suffering wives who are, perhaps, cold and hungry. Moll moralizes a bit, saying that these men are usually very repentant the morning after a night of revelry, but they cannot stand thinking about their plight for long and soon return to drink and bad company. They are hopeless, Moll says, because they have neither principles nor religion to support them.

Comment

This, of course, must be the elderly, experienced Moll who is preaching to us. As a young woman she never had any principles except when it was financially worthwhile, and she never thought about religion until she was condemned to death.

However, Moll finds a widow in the Mint who also dislikes the life there. This woman's husband had been captain of a merchant ship, but had lost his cargo in a storm and died of chagrin. His widow had taken refuge in the Mint because of some debts he had left, but she had been able to settle with her creditors. She suggests that Moll might be able to find a rich captain to marry if she came to live with her.

Comment

Moll has already forgotten any scruples she might have had about entering into a bigamous marriage.

Moll goes to live with the captain's widow, but soon finds that sea captains only marry women who have either money or influence among the merchants to get them a ship to command. This experience confirms what Moll's Colchester sister-in-law maintained about marriage: it is a business arrangement and men are almost entirely influenced in the choice of a wife by the amount of money she can bring them. The captain's widow, however, soon finds a prosperous husband.

Moll also discovers that the men are able to pick and choose, and if one woman should happen to refuse them, have no difficulty in finding another. Some go fortune-hunting quite openly, but do not permit the women to even inquire as to their own wealth. To illustrate this, Moll tells the story of the Redriff lady.

Comment

Redriff was a London suburb inhabited largely by seafaring people.

This young woman, who has a considerable fortune, dares to ask her suitor how much money he has. He quickly stops visiting her. The young lady is quite upset by this, not only because she likes the captain, but because he is now courting another lady who is not as wealthy as she is.

Moll is quite friendly with the young woman and advises her to take revenge on her former suitor by using the power of gossip. She must let it be known that she has dismissed him because he has misrepresented his fortune, has questionable morals, will lose his ship if he cannot find the money to pay for his share in it, and may even have wives in foreign ports. This story spreads quite quickly, to the consternation of the captain, who has told everyone that he is no longer interested in the lady. As a result of the rumors spread about him, he is snubbed by everyone. Finally, as Moll has foreseen the captain begs the young lady to see him once more. When she tells him all the rumors she has "heard," he is astounded and hastens to bring proof that they are false. The result, as Moll predicted, is that the young captain submits to questioning about his character, finances and prospects, but dares not ask the young lady for similar information about herself. She wisely places a good part of her money in trust, so that only she can spend it. The young woman is now the captain's lady, as she wished to be from the beginning.

Comment

The story of the Redriff lady is an example of Defoe's disjointed writing style. It is a digression and has no direct connection with Moll's own story. However, it makes a point which interests Defoe about Marriage.

Moll reflects, after relating this incident, that women in general would be better off if they, like the captain's lady of the story, would take a firm stand with their suitors. She also feels that women should make extensive inquiries about their prospective husbands' fortunes and characters.

Comment

The twice-married, once-widowed young Moll Flanders seems to be learning fast. Yet as we shall see, she does not follow her own good advice.

Adding a denunciation of most men, Moll advises women against marrying the first man who proposes and concludes that nearly every woman can find a good husband if she looks long enough.

Comment

Comments like this one account for the ironic tone of the book. Moll tries five husbands, in addition to other liaisons, before she finds one that suits her.

CHAPTER 4: A NEW HUSBAND WON AND LOST

Moll now continues her own story. She discovers that it is not easy to find a good husband when one is poor.

Comment

This seems to contradict her previous statement concerning the availability of husbands, but it confirms her earlier comment that men are more interested in a woman's fortune than in her appearance or personality.

She therefore decides to move to an area where her poverty is not known. The young woman, whom Moll hereafter refers to as the captain's lady, is grateful to Moll for her assistance in spreading false rumors about the captain and suggests that Moll act as though she were a wealthy widow. The captain's lady assures Moll that since prosperous men are interested in marrying only women who can bring influence or money to the marriage, Moll will be certain to find a rich husband is she pretends she is rich too. Therefore, the captain's lady tells a few people, including her husband, that Moll has an income of fifteen hundred pounds a year, with the possibility of more in the future. She also invites Moll to stay at her new home in a different part of town.

Thus Moll needs to do nothing but wait, while marriageable men flock to see the "rich" young widow. Moll's part in this plot is merely to choose the man who is least likely to doubt the captain's word about her fortune. She, of course, never mentions money to her suitors.

Moll quickly picks out her future husband but decides to test his protestations of love. She continually pretends to doubt his avowals and tells him that he only loves her for her money. He, however, continues to assert that he loves her for herself alone. Finally, one day when he is visiting her, he begins writing on the window with his diamond ring.

Comment

The classic way to determine whether a diamond is real or imitation is to scratch a piece of glass with it. The real diamond will cut into the glass. The idea of writing love letters on glass with a diamond was already a cliche of romantic fiction in Defoe's time. Perhaps the most famous exchange of this sort is that between Elizabeth I and her courtier, Sir Walter Raleigh. Legend has it that Raleigh, as a young man seeking favor at court, scrawled on the glass in Elizabeth's presence, "I hope to climb, but that I fear to fall." In reply the Queen wrote, "If thy heart fails thee, do not climb at all." Romantic as it may be, it is a clumsy method of communication.

They exchange comments by this method, he claiming that he loves her, she asserting that he only loves her money. He finally becomes angry and writes that he loves her alone. This is what Moll has been hoping for; she seizes the opportunity to write that she is poor. By way of reply, the suitor kisses her and, since writing on glass with a diamond is very time consuming, uses pen and paper for his answer. He writes that he wants to marry her despite her poverty and she replies that he hopes she really is rich. Finally he urges, again in writing, that they talk of love rather than of fortunes. Her final sentence, which encourages him greatly, says that it is enough if she does not hate him.

Thus the courtship continues, he protesting his undying love, she constantly telling him of her poverty. Naturally, he does not believe her. Although Moll truthfully states that she is poor, she wants her suitor to think she is as rich as rumor says she is. When they are finally married, he will never be able to reproach her for deceiving him about her wealth.

One of Moll's other tactics consists in ascertaining the degree of his wealth before he can make inquiries about hers. However, she asks her questions subtly, and tells him that he need not answer them. Her suitor is quite frank with her, telling her that he has three plantations in Virginia from which he derives an income of about three hundred pounds a year, but which would be worth more if he lived on them and managed them himself. She tells him that she does not want to go to Virginia but secretly she decides that they will go there as soon after their marriage as possible. He assures her that he will never take her anywhere against her will, and also states that he will not ask her any questions about her own fortune.

Moll points out the skill with which she handles her suitor, making sure that he cannot accuse her of deceit, and seeming almost reluctant to marry him. She emphasizes that there is no necessity to rush into marriage, because the longer the courtship, the more satisfactory the marriage will be. As a result of her careful campaign, her suitor is not too angry when, after the wedding, she tells him exactly how much money she has.

Moll tells us that her suitor became an excellent husband. However, she indicates that she thought him richer than he actually was.

Comment

It is difficult to see why Moll should be disappointed in the income of her third husband. She tells us that he made no secret of his wealth, but a few paragraphs later she indicates that his fortune is less than she anticipated it would be. Either Defoe is inconsistent (as he often is), or the American husband (as we will call him) deliberately exaggerated in order to marry what he thought was a rich widow.

After Moll is married, she patiently waits for her new husband to ask about her fortune. Since he does not mention it, after about two weeks she hesitantly brings up the subject. She tells him that she has heard that Captain _____ has told him she is quite rich; this upsets her because, while she herself (she pointedly reminds him) has never pretended to have any money, she is afraid that he will be angry. Her husband reassures her that she is not at fault, and that if he has been deceived, it has not been by her. Moll craftily presents her husband with a sum of money, telling him that she has a little more. After a few days, she gives him another hundred pounds and a week later, brings the final installment. Her total resources amount to about five hundred pounds, but by bringing him the money in small amounts, she makes him grateful that it is as much as it is, rather than disappointed that she has so little.

> **Comment**

For once, Moll seems to deal honestly with her husband. She tells him that she has given him all her money and, since Defoe gives such exact figures, we know that she has not kept any of it back. Later in her life, Moll will invariably keep some of her funds secret.

Moll then tells her husband that to make up for her lack of fortune, she is willing to go to Virginia with him.

> **Comment**

Moll pretends that she is willing to go to her husband's plantations only because she is upset at his having been told that she is rich. However, we know that she has planned to go to Virginia all along.

Moll's husband tells her that his mother and sister are in Virginia, but they will move to a different house so that Moll will have complete control of her own home. Moll describes the voyage to America in one paragraph, merely commenting that it was very stormy and they were attacked by pirates who not only took most of the goods they had on board, but also threatened to kidnap her husband.

> **Comment**

The voyage to America was lengthy, frequently taking three months. Six weeks was considered a reasonable passage. Moll does not exaggerate the dangers of the journey for the sailing ships sometimes capsized in stormy weather. Pirates were a constant danger.

Moll is quite happy in Virginia, but suddenly she discovers a terribly upsetting fact.

Comment

Defoe builds up a certain amount of suspense by having Moll tell us that something terrible is about to occur, but leading up to the revelation gradually.

Moll's mother-in-law, who has remained in the house at Moll's request, tells her many stories about Virginia and the people living there. The majority of the residents came to Virginia either as indentured servants or as transported criminals. However, once their time is up, these people are permitted to begin farms (or plantations) of their own and many rise to positions of wealth and prestige.

Comment

Many poor people in England, finding no opportunities to better their lot at home, decided to emigrate to the colonies. Since they did not have enough money to pay for their passage, they entered into a contract by which they would have free transportation; in return the ship owner could sell their services to a plantation owner for a period of time (usually seven years). These people were known as indentured servants (or bond-servants) but, as Moll's mother-in-law points out, they were no better off than slaves in many ways. During the period of the contract (or indenture) these people were paid nothing, but had food, lodging and clothing provided for them.

The nature of "transportation" for those convicted of crimes punishable by death has already been discussed. (See Chapter 1.)

Then Moll's mother-in-law tells Moll that she herself was once transported. Showing the brand she bears on her hand, she emphasizes that in Virginia this causes no shame or embarrassment and cites the examples of a major, formerly a pickpocket, and a judge who was once a shoplifter.

Comment

After conviction and prior to transportation, the criminal was branded on the hand (in the same way that cattle are now branded as a means of identification) so that, once he came to America, he would not be able to escape or pretend that he was not a convict. The English penal system used brands for other purposes too. For instance, a person convicted of "seditious libel" could be branded with the initials "S.L." on his cheek. Branding was also common for a number of offenses in the New England colonies. You will recall that in Nathaniel Hawthorne's novel, *The Scarlet Letter*, the minister brands himself with the letter A (for Adulterer).

After several conversations concerning the antecedents of various people in Virginia, Moll asks her mother-in-law about her own history. She tells Moll that in her youth she frequently brought food to a relative who was in Newgate prison and thus came to know many criminals. Her relative was sentenced to death, was reprieved because of pregnancy, but finally died in prison. Moll's mother-in-law, after pausing to condemn the evils of Newgate prison and its bad influence on many people, tells Moll about herself in great detail.

Moll becomes more and more nervous as the story continues and when her mother-in-law mentions her maiden name, Moll nearly faints. However, she excuses her strange reactions by saying the tale has depressed her and then asks her mother-in-law to change the subject. Surprised at this, Moll's mother-in-law comments that at least the story has had a happy ending for when she came to Virginia she was fortunate enough to find a good master. When her mistress died, her employer married her and she had two children. He has been dead for some sixteen years, but since his death, she has continued to improve the estate, which is now much more valuable.

Moll hardly hears the conclusion to her mother-in-law's story, for she realizes that this is her own mother and that her husband is her step-brother. She is expecting her third child and does not know what to do. Characteristically, Moll adds that she wishes she did not know these facts, because then everything would be all right.

Comment

Here we see Moll's (and Defoe's) system of morality: an action is wrong only if you have been told it is wrong. For Moll, there is no such thing as an absolute right and wrong. Thus, the actual crime in her marriage to her half brother consists in her knowledge of their relationship.

Moll is quite upset because she is far from England, knows that her husband will cease living with her once he knows she is his sister, and does not know how she can convince her mother of her identity.

Comment

Moll's first thought naturally concerns her material security. She wants to be sure that she will be accepted as a sister, if not as a wife, so that her husband-brother will continue to support her "in the style to which she has become accustomed."

Despite Moll's avowed horror, she continues this incestuous relationship for another three years. However she says, almost smugly, that she has no more children. Moll's mother continues to tell stories of her younger days, but she seems truly sorry for her former misdeeds. The situation becomes intolerable, for Moll and her husband-brother quarrel frequently. Finally Moll reminds him that when they were first married, he promised that they would return to England if she wished. He, after pleading with her to change her mind and telling her that going to England would be financially disastrous, flatly refuses. Now Moll tells him that if he will not go with her, she will go by herself. This naturally enrages him and he reminds her of her duties as wife and mother. Moll comments to herself that this plea cannot move her since he is really her brother and she does not consider herself his wife.

Comment

We may well ask why Moll ever considered going to England with her husband-brother. One would think that she would be primarily interested in leaving him. It is obvious that Moll really does not care whether she is involved in an incestuous relationship; what bothers her is the prospect of being found out. If she is far away from her mother, no one can ever know, so everything will be all right?

Moll and her husband-brother quarrel constantly and she sometimes uses such strange language that at one point he threatens to have her put in an insane asylum. This upsets her even more, because if she were once accused of insanity, no one would ever believe her strange story. Finally they have so violent an argument that Moll bluntly tells him that he is not her legal husband. This shocks him so much that he becomes ill. When he recovers he questions her closely, believing that perhaps she has a husband already. Moll cannot truthfully deny this, but she refuses to make any further statements.

Moll's husband-brother asks his mother to try to unravel the story, but Moll quickly tells her mother that she is keeping her trouble secret merely out of respect for her. After much discussion and solemn promises of secrecy, Moll tells her mother the facts. It takes all Moll's skill to make her mother believe the story but she finally does, although she several times tries to confuse Moll by changing the facts of her own biography.

In deciding what to do, both Moll and her mother agree that her husband-brother cannot be trusted to keep the matter a secret. They also fear that once he knows the facts he will repudiate both Moll and their children, leaving them in dire poverty. However, Moll notes that while her mother feels she should keep the whole thing a complete secret, continuing to act as wife to her brother, Moll herself has developed a loathing for her brother and does not wish to live with him under any circumstances. She asks her mother to support her in her desire to leave for England and once she is gone, to reveal the relationship to her son, at the same time preventing him from disinheriting the children or remarrying while Moll is alive.

> **Comment**

Moll admits that she is not concerned about the moral issue; she genuinely dislikes her husband-brother. If she did not, she would probably have remained married to him for the rest of her life!

Since the husband-brother is so adamant in refusing to let her leave, Moll decides to tell him of their relationship. Her mother has urged him to be kinder to her, and he is. More important for Moll, he stops talking of sending her to a madhouse. For about a month they get along quite well but one evening as they are talking together, Moll sighs and says she wishes they could continue like this. In response to his urgent questioning, Moll says she cannot tell him the cause of her distress because then he would be unhappy too. He finally agrees to stop urging her to tell him the source of her discomfort but, since this is not what she wants, she says that she will tell him if he will promise, in writing, that he will not blame her either for what she tells him or for not telling him sooner. He must also vow never to discuss the secret with anyone except his mother and to do nothing to harm either Moll or his mother.

When this strange document is signed, Moll tells him that they are brother and sister; he is so upset that he faints. Moll revives him and then tries to calm him. Agreeing that Moll is not at fault, her brother says that she need not go to England. By saying that he is the one who is making the situation awkward, he hints that he can solve everything by committing suicide. Moll comments that although she understands what he means, she does not think he will commit so rash an act because usually the people who talk about suicide never commit it.

Comment

We notice that Moll never tells her husband just when she discovered they were related by blood. Undoubtedly he never suspects that she has known this for over three years.

Although Moll tries to reason with her brother and plan some solution to their difficulties, he persists in his original idea, attempting suicide twice. He becomes seriously ill and Moll wonders if perhaps she should stay in Virginia because if he dies she will be able to remarry there with considerable advantage. However, she decides that she would prefer to go to England and her husband finally agrees to let her return.

Moll and her brother decide that after she has gone, he should pretend that he has received news of her death. Then he can remarry if he wishes. However, they will continue to correspond as brother and sister and he will give her financial support. Moll notes that her brother was not as regular in his financial contributions as she hoped he would be.

CHAPTER 5: MISTRESS MOLL

After eight years in Virginia, Moll finally returns to England. The voyage is quite fast, taking only a month, but they encounter several storms off the coast of England which delay them further. Moll finally leaves the ship (which has temporarily docked in Wales), resolving to go to London by land. The journey overland takes her about three weeks and when she finally gets to London she learns that the ship has reached Bristol after further storms and that some of the cargo has been ruined. This news is quite upsetting, because the bulk of Moll's resources is in merchandise. Now she finds herself with less than three hundred pounds and no friends. Going to Bristol to dispose of those of her goods which are undamaged, she visits Bath and decides to spend the season there.

Comment

Bath, or "the Bath" as Defoe calls it, is the site of natural hot springs. The Romans built baths there (hence the name of this city) in 54 A.D. During the eighteenth century, Bath was an extremely fashionable resort frequented by people who came to "drink the waters" which were considered to have medicinal properties and by even larger numbers of people who came for the social activities. As with any resort, Bath had its "season," the fashionable time of year for staying there. Bath is still visited by invalids (the mineral springs are beneficial for several types of illness) and especially by tourists, who are attracted by the fine eighteenth-century buildings and the Roman baths. The water tastes, as Charles Dickens said, like "warm flat-irons."

Moll has a good time at Bath but finds it very expensive. She also discovers that men come there for entertainment, not to look for wives. Although she realizes that her landlady winks at immorality, Moll conducts herself as a respectable widow and attracts no dishonorable proposals. She remains in Bath for the winter, for she finds that it is less expensive during that season than London is. She tells her landlady that she has suffered a financial loss but expects that her brother in Virginia will make it good.

Few people visit Bath during the winter, but it becomes lively again in the spring. A gentleman whom Moll has met during the fall returns to Bath in the spring and again pays her marked attentions. Moll suspects that her landlady has informed the gentleman of Moll's continued presence there, but both he and the landlady deny this. This gentleman seems completely honorable but Moll realizes he cannot marry her; he already has a wife, though unfortunately she is insane.

After a while the landlady suggests to Moll that the gentleman should give her occasional presents, since he takes up so much of her time. Although Moll denies that she will accept anything, the landlady suggests this idea to the gentleman, who soon begins questioning Moll about her financial circumstances. Moll refuses to tell him anything concrete, merely saying that although she has suffered some losses, she has enough to live on and expects further merchandise when the next Virginia fleet arrives.

Comment

Because of the danger of pirates, merchant ships from the colonies generally traveled together, making up a "fleet." There were two or three sailings a year, but none during the winter months.

The gentleman persists in his questions and finally tells Moll that he wishes to assist her should she need money. Exercising considerable restraint, Moll does not take advantage of the gentleman's offer, a circumstance which rather upsets the scheming landlady. One morning the landlady tells Moll, in the presence of the gentleman, that the messenger Moll sent to Bristol for money has returned empty handed. Indignantly our heroine assures her friend that this is false and shows him the money she has just received from the messenger. She tells him that the landlady is probably concerned about the unpaid rent.

The next morning the gentleman asks Moll to show him all of her money, which she readily does. She does not have very much left after paying the landlady. He then shows her a drawer in which he has a great deal of money and makes her take out a large handful. Placing her own coins in his drawer, he tells her to take the handful of gold to her own room. Moll tells us that he soon begins encouraging her to buy new clothes and when she protests that she must be careful of the money he lent her, informs her that it is a gift. After a short time they set up housekeeping, although their personal relationship remains entirely platonic.

Three months after the beginning of this highly virtuous association, the gentleman becomes seriously ill. Moll nurses him back to health, sitting up with him all night when necessary. He is appropriately grateful and protests his deep affection for her. However he maintains that he has such respect for Moll's virtue that he would not violate her chastity even if they were in bed together.

The Bath gentleman is quite anxious to demonstrate his forbearance to Moll and soon has the opportunity. Traveling to Bristol, they stop at an inn which is so crowded that they cannot obtain separate rooms. Much to Moll's surprise, as she tells us, her friend keeps his promise. For the next two years they live in this unusual way.

Unfortunately Moll cannot stay virtuous for long and one night when they have had a little too much to drink (Moll's excuse), she tells him that she will release him from his promise for that night. The next morning they are both quite contrite, he because he has been unfaithful to his insane wife and she because she is afraid she might be pregnant. He assures her that he will support the child if she has one.

Comment

As we might expect, Moll's chief concern is that she might lose the financial support of the Bath gentleman and be burdened with an unwanted child.

The platonic relationship is now at an end and eventually Moll finds herself expecting a child. The landlady, who is apparently used to such things, makes herself very useful, telling the parish officers that Moll is the wife of a substantial gentleman presently away on business.

Comment

Since the Poor Law required that the parish support any poor person born within its boundaries, the parish officers tried to prevent anyone who might become a pauper from being born in that parish. They sometimes hustled women out of the parish when they were on the verge of giving birth. Pregnant women without visible husbands were naturally looked upon with intense suspicion. Thus the landlady has to assure the parish officers that Moll's fictitious husband is wealthy and that the child will never be a charge on the parish.

As a result of the landlady's tale Moll, under the guise of "my Lady Cleve" has several highly respectable women attend her in childbirth. She points out that this makes the event rather expensive, but the Bath gentleman does not seem to mind.

Comment

At this time children were born at home with a midwife supervising the birth. The women of the neighborhood generally assisted. The midwife was paid and the assisting women received gifts. The size of the fee and the value of the gifts rose in proportion to one's social position. As we shall see later, there were numerous other charges for bedding, the baby's first clothing, the minister's fee for christening the infant and the entertainment for the guests at the christening. Naturally, if one pretended to be "my Lady Cleve," everything had to be the finest and most expensive obtainable.

The Bath gentleman pays for all this without a murmur and Moll carefully overcharges him so that she can put something aside for the future. She tells us that she has managed, one way or another, to amass the small fortune of two hundred guineas. The child turns out to be a boy, which pleases the Bath gentleman. After Moll's convalescence she, the child, a wet-nurse and a maid go to a London suburb where he has rented an apartment for them.

The Bath gentleman continues to visit Moll frequently for the next six years and she has two more children, neither of whom survive. He often expresses his sorrow that they could not maintain their pure relationship but, as Moll tells us, she has no regrets. However, since she knows he cannot marry her, she continues to save as much money as she can.

One day, Moll receives a note from the Bath gentleman that he is quite ill, but since his wife's relatives are taking care of him, she cannot see him. Two weeks go by during which Moll receives no further notes from her lover. Finally, hearing that he is critically ill, she disguises herself as a servant and goes to his home, pretending to have been sent by a neighbor to inquire after his health. She finds that the doctors have given up all hope, and returns home in despair. She is glad she has saved so much money, but worried that her son, now five years old, will be without support.

Comment

After living with the Bath gentleman for eight years, Moll is sad not because he is dying, but because he is dying without providing for her and the child!

During the next two weeks, Moll sends messengers frequently and finds that he is slowly improving. After a while, she learns that he has fully recovered. However, he does not answer her letters. Four months go by; she writes again and finally has a letter delivered to him personally. The Bath gentleman at last replies and Moll discovers that a previous letter of his never reached her. It seems that during his illness he decided that he should end his illicit relationship with her. In his letter, he sends her some money and tells her to go back to Bath. He informs her that he does not wish to see her again but that he will take care of the child.

Now Moll has some pangs of conscience, remembering that she is still married to the linen-draper and thus has been committing adultery. Expressing contrition at the part she has played in undermining the Bath gentleman's virtue, Moll at the same time worries about how she will provide for herself. She decides not to go to Bath because she is afraid her former landlady will be a bad influence and also, as she frankly admits, because she does not want her to know that she has been "cast off."

Moll then writes to the Bath gentleman, agreeing not to see him and also asking him to send her another fifty pounds so that she can return to her mother in Virginia. She adds that although she will leave her son for his father to take care of, she will, if possible, send for him from Virginia. She also offers to sign a statement releasing him from any further claims other than that of supporting the child. The Bath gentleman readily sends Moll the money and the release to sign. Moll tells us that she has no intention of going to Virginia, but merely wants to get as much money from her former lover as possible.

Moll does, at this point, express affection for her child, but she does it tersely and never mentions him again. She concludes her recital of this **episode** with a moralistic speech on the dangers of trusting good resolutions too far.

CHAPTER 6: IN WHICH THE DECEIVER IS DECEIVED

Moll finds herself at loose ends once more. Despite her previous brief contrition at being a mistress while her second husband presumably still lived, she again feels that she has no obligation toward him and can marry again if she wishes. She is in a fair financial position, having close to five hundred pounds including the second shipment of tobacco which she has induced her brother to send her. However, she is now forty-two and no longer as attractive as she was in her youth. Moll lets it be known that she has a fortune, but finds the lack of friends a distinct disadvantage in her search for a prosperous mate. She comments that a woman without friends and advisers is apt to be deceived; she knows what she wants but does not know how to go about obtaining it. Her chief aim is to find a good husband who will give her a secure position for the rest of her days. Moll adds that had she found such a man before, she would have remained a faithful wife for the rest of her life. She remarks that she never deceived any of her husbands; it was always necessity which led her from the path of virtue.

Comment

Moll's account of herself here seems correct. Her search for security was always directed toward matrimony (she conveniently forgot any previous commitments) and it was only when she failed to find a husband that she tried less honest ways of earning a living.

Moll anxiously awaits the arrival of a likely suitor, but none comes and she finds herself spending her money with no prospect of replacing it. However, a lady who lodges in the same house so extols the low cost of living in the North of England that Moll one day tells her that she may go there herself. The north-country lady repeatedly invites Moll to come with her on a visit to Lancashire which she plans to make shortly and tells her that she has a sister and brother who live near Liverpool and that the brother also has a large estate in Ireland.

Moll comments that the poor woman thought she had three or four thousand pounds and would never have been so friendly if she had known Moll's true circumstances. For her part, Moll tells us that she is in such a desperate situation that she is willing to try anything. Thus, after a great show of reluctance, Moll accepts the north-country woman's invitation and prepares to leave with her. Now, however, she finds herself confronted with the problem of what to do with the money she still has. She does not wish to take it with her, for fear of highwaymen, but knows no one whom she can trust with it. Finally she decides to go to a bank where she has found an honest teller.

> **Comment**

In the eighteenth century, banking was not the reputable business it is today. There were many small banks which could fail at any time leaving the depositors empty handed. Many people deposited their money with moneylenders, but as Moll has already found out, these were inclined to go bankrupt too.

Moll asks the bank teller for advice; he tells her that while he cannot assist, her he has a friend who can. He assures Moll that this friend, who is a clerk in another bank, is scrupulously honest. Moll meets the bank clerk, likes him and hears nothing but good about him. She tells him that she does not know what to do with her money and he explains the various alternatives open to her.

Moll trusts the bank clerk so well that she asks him to act as her steward. She tells him that although she cannot afford to pay him a salary, she has no heirs so the money will be his if she should die. He reluctantly accepts her commission and then comments that he wishes he were a bachelor. Moll remonstrates at this insult to his wife but the bank clerk tells her that his wife has been unfaithful on numerous occasions. Moll advises him to get a divorce, but he claims that this is a lengthy and expensive process.

> **Comment**

Divorce laws were quite strict in the eighteenth century; the only grounds were desertion or adultery. One had to go before an ecclesiastical court to obtain the divorce and since this court also handled other matters, such as disputes about wills, there was a considerable backlog of cases. The legal fees were also considerable.

Moll hints that perhaps he could find a good woman without offering her marriage, if the situation were explained to her. She reflects that she herself would be only too glad to take such an offer. The clerk asserts, however, that it would be very hard to find an honest woman who would be interested in such a proposition, and he has had enough of the other kind. He then asks Moll if she would accept such a proposal. At this point, of course, she cannot accept without branding herself as a woman of easy virtue, and she refuses him in a huff. He then asks if she will have him if he obtains an official divorce. She answers that no woman can answer such a question in advance and begs him not to make mock of her. The bank clerk assures her that he is perfectly serious; he will have her or no one.

The next time she visits him he insists on seeing her home; this disturbs Moll a little, for she suspects that he wants to inquire into her background, but she recalls that her present neighbors know nothing to her disadvantage. In an aside she points out to her readers how important it is for women to be thought respectable, even if they are not. He presses his suit vigorously and swears that he fell in love with Moll the moment he saw her. Moll thinks to herself that it matters little enough when he began to love her, if only he will keep on doing so.

Comment

The **irony** of this situation, with the clerk's calf-like sincerity and Moll's worldly-wise asides to herself makes this one of Defoe's most effective humorous passages. Moll does not often show this consciousness of the gulf between what she pretends to be and what she is; usually she is such a good actress that she is convinced herself of the reality of her pose of the moment.

The clerk will take no denial, and Moll coyly pretends to prepare to leave. At this he calms down; if she considers his offer an insult, he adds, he will say no more about it. This is not the way Moll wants the game to go at all, so she hastily protests that she is willing to hear anything that she can in decency listen to. He proposes that she marry him at once, but they will not live together until the divorce is obtained. Moll's heart says yes to this idea, but the more calculating part of her nature makes her pretend to be insulted. He then suggests that they sign a contract agreeing to marry after the divorce is obtained. This idea is more sensible than the last, Moll admits, and she agrees to consider it.

The reason our heroine does not settle things with the bank clerk then and there is that she has determined to try her fortune in Lancashire. She can come back to the bank clerk if nothing better offers.

The trip to Lancashire is pleasant and the friend's brother, who brings a coach to meet them, seems agreeable. After a stay at a well-to-do merchant's house in Liverpool, they move on to an uncle's large country estate. The only thing Moll finds surprising is that the family are Roman Catholics. However, she admits that she is not one to scruple about religious differences. She attends their religious observances and gives them some hope that she will be converted.

Comment

At this time in England Roman Catholics were discriminated against in a number of ways. They were not allowed to vote or hold public office, they could not attend the universities or enter a profession and (at one time) were not permitted to carry on a business in and live within ten miles of London.

Moll is told that the brother has an estate in Ireland (hence she calls him the Irishman) worth fifteen hundred pounds a year. Her friend, out of a natural capacity for exaggeration, and not at Moll's prompting, tells her brother that Moll is a great heiress with an estate of fifteen thousand pounds. He inquires no further, but carries on a furious and expensive courtship of Moll. His behavior is completely that of the wealthy landed gentleman, and he talks of his lands, his horses and his tenants until Moll is genuinely impressed. The Irishman promises to settle six hundred pounds a year on Moll when they come to Ireland and before long they are married by a Catholic priest.

Moll feels a little badly at abandoning the faithful bank clerk, but the vision of her new wealth soon puts him out of her mind. After they have been married for several weeks her husband begins to talk about returning to Ireland and they go to the town of Chester on the way to the Holyhead boat. The Irishman offers to find them a private lodging, but Moll says that an inn will do for a night or two. They accordingly put up at one; Moll says that she forgets what sign it was at.

Comment

All English inns, of course, were (and still are) identified by the signs hanging outside. Among innumerable prosaic signs like the "Rising Sun" and "Royal George," there were more intriguing ones like the "Turk's Head," the "Goat and Compasses," and the famous London inn which still exists, the "Elephant and Castle." This last is supposed to be the result of the corruption through the centuries of its original name, the "Infanta of Castile"!

Moll's statement that she forgets what the name of the inn was is a typical trick used by Defoe to achieve a realistic effect. When she honestly and understandably says that she forgets one detail, we are all the more ready to believe the details our heroine does remember.

Here her husband reminds Moll that she should look after any administrative details regarding her estate before they cross to Ireland. Moll pretends to be surprised and says she does not know what estate he is talking about. She calls in the sister and asks what she has been telling her brother about his new wife. The sister says she heard in London that Moll had a great fortune and told her brother as much. At this Moll pretends to be very angry and says that her husband has been deceived, but she has had no hand in it. The Irishman breaks out in a furious rage at his sister. (Moll has carefully arranged that his anger will not be directed at her.) He tells Moll that the woman is not his sister at all, but his mistress, that they plotted together to get Moll as his wife on the sister's assurance of her wealth, and that he has no money of his own at all, but has spent what little he had in courting Moll. He is so enraged that the female accomplice fears for her life and escapes in the confusion.

The prospect of the newlyweds is now dismal. Moll is genuinely upset, for she likes her new husband and feels that they would be very happy were it not for this lack of money. They become quite emotional over their sad fate, but Moll is not so carried away that she forgets to conceal a note for thirty pounds or the rest of her stock in London. All she shows her husband is a total of a bit over thirty pounds; she feels she will have had a lucky escape from this adventure if that is all she loses. The next morning when Moll wakes he has gone, leaving ten guineas out of the little money he has left, his gold watch, some jewelry and a note which bids her good-bye forever. At this Moll is extremely upset and spends the day in dejection.

Comment

Despite Moll's attraction to her husband she never considers revealing her own financial resources to him and proposing that they try to get along on that. Apparently she has already learned that she must depend on no one but herself.

After dinner Moll becomes so distraught that she calls aloud for Jemmie, saying that she will give him everything, beg or starve, if only he will come back.

Comment

This is the first time that the name of the husband has been mentioned.

That evening, to Moll's great surprise, he returns. He could not leave, he says, without seeing her again. Moll tells him how she has been calling for him and Jemmie replies that he heard her voice, using exactly those words, when he was twelve miles from the town and even though he saw her running after him. Moll is first amused that he should use such expressions, and then amazed when he swears it is literally true.

Comment

Accounts of supernatural occurrences were very popular in Defoe's day, as they still are to a lesser extent. Defoe himself was very much interested in the appearance of spirits and their actions, and wrote a famous pamphlet about such a happening, called *The Apparition of Mrs. Veal*. The apparition was a hoax, though Defoe probably did not know this when he wrote the pamphlet, and it remains one of the most circumstantial and convincing ghost stories on record.

They are both so reluctant to part that James (or Jemmie) accompanies Moll for most of her trip. When they come within thirty miles of London, he says that it is not "convenient" for him to come any closer, for reasons that it is not necessary to tell her. Moll wonders at this, but has no choice in the matter.

| Comment

Moll finds out much later in the book that he does not want to approach London for fear of being recognized. He is a highwayman.

She implores him to stay with her at the inn at which they have stopped, telling him that she has something of importance to say which she has not yet revealed. Finding a convenient opportunity, she tells him of her previous career in Virginia, and her experience with plantations, though she says that her husband there has been dead for some time. She then explains the nature of planting and describes how with a small investment hard-working people can prosper there.

| Comment

We find repeatedly in Defoe's books that the characters give a "full and distinct account" of some process or place. Here Defoe's

didactic inclination, his interest in instructing his readers, comes out. *Robinson Crusoe* provides the most elaborate and intriguing example of this technique; there we are told in great detail just how Crusoe does everything, from growing grain to making pottery. In the eighteenth century, when most people did not themselves produce most of their own daily needs, this idea of complete self-sufficiency was a fascinating one and provided, as it still does, a great deal of the excitement of *Robinson Crusoe*.

Moll expands on this idea at great length. Jemmie revolves the proposal in his mind and then comes up with an alternative. They can do almost as well for themselves in Ireland. He proposes to go over and try it and if he succeeds, to send for Moll. At this Moll is terrified that he will take her at her word and carry her stock of money with him, but he is too honest to suggest this. The best compromise that Moll can exact is that he will try the Irish venture and if it does not succeed, he will agree to go to America with her. We conclude that they must have talked everything over very thoroughly, for Moll says that the discussions lasted almost a month!

They now part and Moll takes lodgings in London; the pleasant memories of her husband are somewhat shattered when she finds that she is going to have another child. The matter causes her some worry, for unwed mothers were likely to be expelled by the parish officers who did not want the expense of caring for the illegitimate child. Her landlady introduces her to a midwife who runs a kind of hostel for unwed mothers. Moll protests that she has a husband, but her delicacy is lost on the midwife.

Her business is to shelter people like Moll until the baby arrives, she declares, and whether Moll has a husband or not is no concern of hers. She has a sliding scale of charges, in accordance with the wealth of the prospective mother, and everything is done in such a businesslike way that Moll suspects this to be a large-scale operation. She brings Moll three different bills, which are reproduced in the book, all carefully itemized as to food and lodging, servants, the midwife's fees, christening and christening supper.

The prospect of having everything taken care of cheers Moll up immensely. She is very comfortable under the midwife's care, and finds it hard to believe that the woman can make any money when she provides for her patients so well. Her hostess replies that she makes her profit on volume, and our heroine finds that there are indeed a great many other women in her own predicament.

Comment

It is in passages like this one that we can see Defoe's attempt to make *Moll Flanders* a kind of expose of underworld life. Despite the repeatedly emphasized moral purpose of the book, contemporary readers obviously also enjoyed reading about the colorful rackets of eighteenth-century London, such as this example of the "baby-racket."

At this juncture Moll again hears from her bank clerk; he has obtained a divorce from his wife, and since she soon after committed suicide, he is free to marry again. Our heroine now has to stall for time; she urges him to consider very carefully whether he really wants to marry. The child is now born, a fine, healthy boy, but Moll wonders what she will do with him if she marries the bank clerk.

The midwife sees Moll's disturbance and asks her what the trouble is. At first the new mother is reluctant to explain, but at last she describes the situation. The midwife tells her that she is worrying about nothing; the child must be given to someone else to care for. Moll is frightened at this prospect, for she feels that most of the children so disposed of are mistreated and starved, if not actually murdered. In a rather inappropriate aside, she reflects on what children need in the way of proper care, and the sad fate of orphans and abandoned children.

Comment

Defoe repeatedly expresses his concern in this way with the fate of children who lack parents. At the very beginning of *Moll Flanders*, Moll herself reflects that she might never have been guided to a life of crime if she had been properly cared for as a child. Among Defoe's many proposals for social betterment are a number concerning the care of orphan children.

To allay her fears, the midwife tells her that the foster mothers she engages are thoroughly reliable; it is their trade, and thus they have a reputation to lose if the children under their care do not do well. At this Moll is reassured, and for a small extra payment she arranges to visit the child while keeping her own identity concealed. The financial arrangements are concluded and Moll is free again.

CHAPTER 7: AN OLD SUITOR BECOMES A NEW HUSBAND

Now that her child has been provided for, Moll writes to the bank clerk again and finds, to her pleasure, that he is still interested in her. While she has actually been in London all the time, Moll has given the clerk the impression that she has been staying in Liverpool. In his enthusiasm, the clerk proposes to meet her on the way, two days' journey from town. So as not to disillusion him, Moll travels to a place called Stone in Cheshire. She knows no one in the town but as she says, " ... with money in the pocket one is at home anywhere" and after staying a few days she starts back to London. She writes to the clerk to tell him when she is "returning."

In her usual circumstantial way, Moll explains that she is not traveling on one of the regular stages, but in a coach which had been privately hired and was now returning to London, picking up chance passengers but not keeping to any regular schedule.

Comment

There were various methods of overland transportation during this period, all of them comparatively slow and some of them downright painful. Where the roads were in bad condition, and nearly everywhere during the winter, men rode on horseback and ladies did not travel at all. Where the roads were not too bad, there were several other possibilities. The rich, of course, had their own coaches, which were usually elaborately upholstered and decorated and equipped with a coachman and footmen in livery (that is, the uniform of the employer). It was the ambition of every up-and-coming young merchant in London, and still more so of their wives, to have their own coach. Defoe had his coach at a comparatively early age as a result of some fortunate investments, but lost it with everything else at his bankruptcy. Those who could not afford their own coaches, and this included the vast majority of Englishmen, had several choices open to them, depending on the amount of money they were willing to spend. One could hire a private coach for short or long trips.

This is what Moll and her second husband do on their frivolous excursion to Oxford. It was expensive, but one did not have to mix with the vulgar crowd. The most common method of transportation was the regular stagecoach service which ran from London to all parts of England. These stagecoaches were slow (they averaged about ten miles an hour if they were lucky) but dependable and kept to a fairly rigid schedule. The schedule was useful for those traveling on business, but also for the highwaymen, who could figure out just when to meet the coach as it crossed a lonely moor.

The bank clerk meets Moll with a "gentleman's coach and four horses" just outside London. His extravagance is a measure of his love for her. Instead of continuing to London, the clerk insists that they stop overnight at an inn. They take a walk to see the town, the local church and the countryside.

Comment

We can guess that this was Defoe's own custom when he stopped at a new place during his many travels about England and Scotland. His circumstantial descriptions in letters and in the Tour thro' the Whole Island of England and Scotland derive from his observations.

Moll soon enough guesses what is in the wind, for her lover inquires of the innkeeper about a parson. He implores her to marry him immediately, and though Moll makes some objections for form's sake, she does not feel in any position to remonstrate too far. In his thoroughly systematic way the clerk sets to rest what he imagines to be Moll's objections. He shows her the decree of divorce from his previous wife, together with written testimony that she was unfaithful. There is also her death certificate, proof that her death was a suicide, the verdict of the coroner's jury, and even the burial papers!

Comment

It is often difficult to tell when Defoe intends to be humorous, but here we cannot avoid the feeling that he is making fun of the bank clerk's methodical nature. The clerk is supposed to be on fire with passion, but he still thinks in terms of deeds and death certificates! The **irony** of the situation adds to the humor. Moll is prepared to accept him without any papers at all; she is only too glad to find a husband.

Moll consents to the wedding while bemoaning (privately) that her past life has made her so unworthy of this honest man. The parson is very cooperative and consents to marry them upon the spot, at night, in the inn, with the landlord giving the bride away.

Comment

Defoe, as a Dissenter, was not very friendly to the clergymen of the Established Church. Here he points out the willingness of one of them to perform what is obviously a clandestine marriage.

The next morning, while they are still at the inn, Moll is frightened to see Jemmie, her Lancashire husband, going into a neighboring tavern with two other men. Her fears that he is looking for her are allayed when a hue-and-cry follows. All three are wanted as highwaymen for robbing two coaches.

Comment

The hue-and-cry was a method of apprehending criminals in the absence of an effective police force in England. The victim or anyone who observed a crime cried "Stop, thief!" or whatever was appropriate, and at the sound all honest men were required to join in the chase and help to catch the criminal. Later in the book Moll herself is often enough the object of the hue-and-cry.

Moll throws the pursuers off the track by saying that she saw the men and knows one of them to be an honest gentleman. Though she says that she does not know the truth of the matter, she obviously has her suspicions about her recent husband Jemmie.

For five years the new marriage proceeds happily, but then the clerk is thrown into bankruptcy as a result of putting too much trust in an associate. He becomes melancholy and dies under this blow, and Moll is once more left alone. She reflects that she is past her youth and can no longer expect anyone to keep her as a mistress, or to court her as a wife without a fortune, which she does not have.

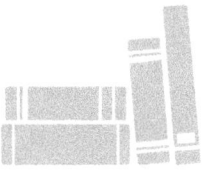

MOLL FLANDERS

TEXTUAL ANALYSIS

PART II: THE DISREPUTABLE DEEDS OF MOLL FLANDERS

CHAPTER 8: POVERTY LEADS TO CRIME

For two years Moll lives upon her small capital, fearing that destitution is just around the corner. She reminds her readers that temptation is greatest at the moments of worst distress. At last, as she wanders the London streets disconsolately, she sees a bundle lying untended in an open shop.

Comment

In the seventeenth and eighteenth centuries, shops and taverns usually had folding doors in front and were more or less wide open to the street during business hours. This was, of course, long before the time of plate glass, and an open shop-front was the only way for the tradesman to display his wares. It is because the shops are half open that Moll is able to look in and see everything that is going on. Most tradesmen had one or two apprentices standing in the shop to wait on customers and also to prevent the pilfering of people like Moll. But the apprentices were only boys (or girls) after all; they were notoriously muddleheaded and easily distracted.

This passage provides a typical example of Defoe's use of circumstantial detail to achieve a realistic effect. Moll sees the package, "... as I passed by an apothecary's shop in Leadenhall Street." London readers probably knew just the spot the author had in mind.

Moll can almost hear the devil telling her to take the bundle, and she does so. The horror of this new crime, and the risk, nearly overwhelm her, and she runs off, hardly knowing where she is going. When she has recovered somewhat she opens the package and finds a number of valuable pieces of silverware, as well as some linen and silk, and nearly a pound in money. Fear of capture torments her, as well as the thought that these things may have been taken from someone even poorer than herself. However, she goes out again and meets a little girl returning alone from a dancing class. She lures the child into an alley and takes the gold necklace she is wearing without the victim knowing it.

She is less concerned about this second robbery, for she feels it is a lesson to the parents not to let their daughter wander about alone, and a reproof to their vanity for letting the child wear such an expensive piece of jewelry.

Comment

Moll's remark that the **episode** will teach the parents a lesson is one example of her ability to excuse her misdeeds. It was part of the Puritan state of mind (though not confined to them) to justify their more dubious actions in this way.

Now that she has definitely entered upon a career of crime, Moll takes up the business with a will. Her inexperience, however, prevents her from realizing as large a profit as she hopes for. Still, the devil (as she maintains) puts a number of lucky opportunities in her way. One evening a man pursued by the hue-and-cry runs past her and drops part of his booty near where she is standing. She stands in front of it until the pursuit is past and then takes the bundle home with no risk to herself. When she opens it she finds a large piece of silk and a whole bolt of velvet, both of which are quite valuable. Her conscience bothers her very little over this escapade, for she rationalizes to herself that she has only robbed a thief.

As she gains confidence, Moll enlarges her field of activities to the suburbs around London. Near Stepney she sees two rings lying on the window sill of a private house. Cleverly, she raps on the window to see if anyone is within earshot. If someone answers, she intends to tell them to take the rings away, for she has seen two men looking at them in a suspicious manner. No one responds, so she breaks the window and makes off with the rings; one is a diamond ring worth three pounds, the other much less valuable.

Moll has now expanded her activities to such an extent that she has trouble disposing of the stolen goods and suspects that she is not being paid what they are worth. In short, she needs a reliable fence. In this predicament, her thoughts turn to her old midwife, who can be assumed to have useful underworld contacts. Apparently the business of caring for unwed mothers is not what it has been; her friend has been in trouble with the law over one of her boarders and is now very poor. The midwife is still energetic, however, and has turned "pawnbroker." Moll tells her that she has run out of money but still has some goods left, and the woman agrees to sell them for her. At this the heroine asks if she can help her to some kind of lawful occupation; the answer she receives is the occasion for one of Moll's numerous ironic remarks to the reader. "But here she was deficient: honest business did not come within her reach." We can imagine to ourselves the stress Moll puts on the word, "honest." If she had been younger, she continues, the midwife might have found a gentleman friend for her, but Moll has given up hopes of "that kind of livelihood."

At length the midwife invites Moll to come and stay at her house. Moll tries to find sewing to do, "but that was very hard to do for one that had no manner of acquaintance in the world."

Comment

Defoe was a hard-headed though unsuccessful businessman. He understands, and here makes clear to his readers, how important "connections" are, even in so small a matter as making a living as a seamstress (a woman who does needlework).

Eventually Moll does find work for her needle and manages to make barely enough to live on, but the much easier life of crime still attracts her. As she is walking through the streets with eyes open for anything that may turn up, she happens to look into an inn and sees a silver tankard (a tall mug, often with a hinged lid) on a table. She sits down at the table and orders a drink of ale. There are a number of serving boys going in and out, and in the confusion Moll is able to pretend that the tankard belongs to her. She finishes her drink and walks out with it.

Comment

The fact that Moll can steal a tankard so easily needs some explanation. At this time, silver and pewter drinking cups were quite expensive and taverns usually owned only a few. It was quite common for people to carry their own mugs with them; this ensured that they would have one when they wanted a drink without having to wait until someone else had finished. At the same time, bringing your own tankard guaranteed that it was clean; innkeepers made only the sketchiest efforts to wash their tableware. Thus no one is surprised at the idea that Moll has brought her own mug and as she explains, the boys think that all the inn's tankards are accounted for. One of Defoe's great literary assets is illustrated here. He presents strikingly realistic pictures of contemporary life by the use of a few details. In this scene we feel that we are standing behind Moll, looking over her shoulder into the inn. This kind of naturalistic picture of everyday life is very rare in English literature before Defoe's time.

The time has come, Moll now feels, to find out whether the midwife can be trusted as an accomplice. She explains how she has "accidentally" brought away a tankard that does not belong to her and asks what she should do. Should she take it back? We can imagine that Moll is not very surprised to hear her friend tell her that she must do no such thing. The innkeeper is only too likely to accuse her of having stolen it and a number of others as well. Besides, she says, your need is greater than theirs.

| Comment

Here we see Defoe providing an example of "natural law" at work. According to natural law, people reduced to an extremity are justified in taking from those who have more than they need. This theoretical "law of necessity," however, applies to cases of actual starvation, not to those who are merely poor, like Moll. She and her colleague simply use it as an excuse for their illegal actions.

It is not very long before Moll discovers that people bring her friend all sorts of stolen goods to dispose of; she is a fence after all. She melts down the tankard so that it cannot be traced and gives Moll the full value of the silver, although she cheats the others who deal with her. When Moll complains about her lack of skill at stealing, the midwife introduces her to a friend who is a "specialist." This woman deals in shoplifting, stealing pocketbooks and watches.

| Comment

At this time women wore their watches, which were expensive and rather uncommon, hooked to the waist or bosom of their dresses; presumably this was done both for convenience and display. Defoe is constantly pointing out how silly such customs are; an incidental purpose of the book is to demonstrate the practices of shoplifters and pickpockets like Moll and her friends so that people can safeguard themselves against them. One of his many pamphlets is entitled *An Effectual Scheme for the Immediate Prevention of Street Robberies*.

Admiring her skill, Moll decides to take lessons from her. After some practice, they decide to try their luck on a real victim and select a pregnant woman who is coming down the steps of a church. The accomplice pretends to fall against her, and as the woman tries to save herself, Moll slips her watch off undetected and makes off. The watch is a valuable one and the midwife allows them twenty pounds for it, of which the newly graduated pickpocket gets half.

Comment

Moll is always very precise about the value of things-it is part of her rather mercenary character.

At this point Moll observes that once she is driven to crime by necessity, there is an irresistible temptation to continue with it, even though she is no longer destitute. She has become hardened to wrongdoing and her partners encourage her. Moll does consider leaving the trade, for she has accumulated nearly two hundred pounds, but avarice and the devil keep her at it, and she concludes that fate is too strong for her. She has the gambler's instinct to keep on until she has a really large sum.

Comment

It is always difficult to distinguish Moll's thoughts at the time from the observations made in her old age as she tells her story. This is something of a flaw in Defoe's technique. In the passage just concluded we probably have a mixture of the two. Probably she did consider giving up her criminal career, but the philosophical reflections she makes sound like the product of her mature judgment.

Caught in the act of stealing some cloth, Moll's instructor in the art of picking pockets and another pupil are convicted and condemned to die. They "plead their bellies" (say that they are pregnant) and the sentence is delayed. Moll visits the prisoners for a while, but soon finds it too depressing. This is, after all, the place of her own birth! Besides, though she does not say so, she is too self-centered to feel sorry for others for very long. The teacher is finally executed.

This terrible example deters the heroine for a while, but an irresistible opportunity presents itself. There is a fire in a neighboring house, and in the confusion Moll makes off with a collection of valuables which the householders are trying to save. The thought that she has deprived these people of the little they thought to save moves even Moll's hardened conscience, but she cannot bring herself to give back any of her loot and soon forgets her remorse.

Both the midwife (whom Moll calls her "governess") and Moll herself are alarmed by the execution of Moll's instructor and behave more cautiously for a while. Moll scores on some easy marks who have just set up their shop. Such people, she observes wisely, are always targets for the shoplifter until they have learned to be more suspicious through sad experience. No opportunities offer themselves for some time, and Moll thinks again of giving up her career. Her "governess," however, who does not wish to lose such a dependable supplier of stolen goods, puts her in touch with a young couple in the same line of business. Moll, who is now an expert, finds their methods crude and turns down several of their more foolhardy proposals. They attempt to rob a watchmaker without her, are caught, tried and executed.

At her governess's instigation Moll now turns her hand to a new occupation, that of informer. She tells Moll where a large quantity of smuggled Flemish lace is to be found. Going to the customs officer, Moll offers to lead him to the lace in return for a share of the reward. When they arrive, she manages to hide a good proportion of the lace in her clothing, and so makes a double profit.

Comment

So many luxuries, such as tobacco, tea and coffee, wines, brandy and lace, were subject to high import duties at this period that a large smuggling trade flourished. The twenty-mile-wide English Channel, with France on the other side, presented a temptation to any seaman with a fast boat and a taste for adventure. The customs officers were paid largely on commission, in proportion to the value of the smuggled goods they seized, and naturally they were willing to split their reward with an informer in return for a good haul.

The officer tries to cheat Moll out of her due, but she is a sharp bargainer and clears about a hundred pounds on the transaction.

A little later Moll makes another attempt at a woman's gold watch. This time the watch is firmly attached and she is in danger of being discovered. Moll, who is well-dressed, quickly pushes on through the crowd and calls out, "A pickpocket!" before her intended victim has a chance to and so draws suspicion away from herself. There really is another pickpocket in the crowd and he is caught and lynched.

Comment

The sense of life, of hustle and bustle, the pressure of the crowd and its rage, make this one of Defoe's best scenes. Again he relies on evocative details. At the same time we can see one of his weaknesses in the same passage. After telling how the second pickpocket is caught by the crowd, he continues with a long digression on how criminals prefer this treatment to languishing in Newgate Prison with the certainty of hanging or transportation. This misplaced aside destroys the immediacy of the scene and weakens its impact.

Defoe again uses this occasion to tell his readers how to guard themselves against pickpockets; they must turn around immediately when they feel the pull and grab the person nearest to them. A short history of her governess now interrupts the story. Moll then continues that she is so successful at eluding capture that she arouses the jealousy of her fellow-thieves; it is at this point that they first give her the name of Moll Flanders, which has no connection with her real name.

To avoid being betrayed by her former accomplices, Moll dresses as a man for a time, but a narrow escape convinces her that the unfamiliar costume is too clumsy. She is pursued to her governess's house and the house is searched. But since Moll has changed back to woman's clothes and the searchers are looking for a man, she is not suspected.

Moll's male accomplice who is captured in this latest burglary tries to inform on her but fails because he is unaware of her female identity. Moll is nevertheless very nervous and leaves the city until she hears the "joyful news" that he has been hanged. She goes to an inn where she and Jemmie stayed previously, and the solicitous inquiries of her landlady, who knows nothing about her criminal career, about her "husband" provide an ironic counterpoint to Moll's own worries. Upon her return, she resolves to play a lone hand and trust no longer to "honor among thieves."

CHAPTER 9: A PROFITABLE ENCOUNTER

Despite all these narrow escapes, as well as the fact that she has accumulated the tidy fortune of five hundred pounds, our heroine cannot bring herself to give up her unlawful career. In spite of her resolve, she takes a young woman as partner and is aghast to see her arrested in possession of goods Moll has stolen. Moll congratulates herself on the fact that she has not revealed her identity or her lodging to this girl. She is relieved when the accomplice is transported, both because she has escaped the death penalty and also because she is now too far away to be a witness against Moll herself. Moll sounds rather cold blooded when she remarks: "I was now easy as to all fear of witnesses against me, for all those that had either been concerned with me, or that knew me by the name of Moll Flanders, were either hanged or transported." She may be a skillful thief, but she seems to be a jinx to her companions in crime.

At another fire Moll is standing in the street, wondering if she can repeat her previous success, when she is almost killed by a feather-bed thrown from an upper window. Although knocked unconscious and bruised, she receives no permanent injury.

Comment

Fires were a constant danger in the crowded, shoddily built London of the seventeenth and eighteenth centuries. What primitive fire-fighting equipment there was could hardly make its way through the twisted streets. At just about the time at which Moll's story is supposed to take place, in 1666, more than half the city was burned to the ground in what became known as the Great Fire of London. The catastrophic fire had a fortunate side effect; it destroyed the nesting places of rats and thus ended serious outbreaks of the Plague.

As a person whose thinking has the fundamentalist cast of Puritanism, Moll is inclined to attribute accidental events like this one to direct Divine intervention. She comments stoically, however, that she is "reserved for further afflictions."

It is the time of year when Bartholomew Fair is held, and Moll visits it to see what may offer, without any real expectation of success.

Comment

The great fairs in England were the social high point of the year for the common people. A number of towns each had its annual fair (held at different times of the year) where merchants would come from all over the country and abroad to set up booths and sell their wares. London had three or four fairs during the year. They were something like the American state fairs, but with more emphasis on buying and selling. The heyday of the fairs was the Middle Ages, when people bought a good deal of their necessities for the year at them. By Defoe's time they had declined and were given over to cheap merchandise, popular entertainments like bear-baiting and cock-fighting, and as Defoe points out, gambling. (The word "tawdry" is derived from St. Audrey's Fair, where particularly cheap ornaments were sold.)

In one of the gambling parlors she meets a gentleman rather far gone in drink. He first takes her to the Spring Garden, where he drinks some more.

Comment

The "gardens" of eighteenth-century London were semi-public places (they sometimes charged admission) where the upper classes went to "take the air" and to walk and meet their friends. There were stalls where one could buy tea or something stronger, and often a pavilion for dancing. Vauxhall Gardens, Spring Garden and Ranelagh were among the most famous, and each was the favorite of fashionable people for a brief period. As the gardens declined they drew a lower-class clientele and became rather notorious as a place of resort for prostitutes.

They then go to a kind of low hotel and Moll yields herself to him without much argument. As they are returning in a coach, drink gets the better of the man and Moll takes the opportunity to lift all his valuables, which are considerable, and escape as the coach stops momentarily. Moll makes this adventure the occasion for a homily on the perils of drunkenness; it overthrows virtue and reason together, and she quotes Solomon to clinch her point.

When Moll relates the incident to her governess, she is able to identify the man. The two drive a good trade by selling back to him his expensive gold watch, sword and periwig.

Comment

All gentlemen wore elaborate wigs, some of which were quite expensive. This one is valued at sixty guineas, which is sixty-three pounds.

It develops that the gentleman is not so much angry at being robbed as he is afraid of catching a disease. The governess, who acts as go-between, assures him that he is in no danger from Moll, and at this he brightens up considerably and asks to see her again. Eventually he and Moll come to an agreement, and he visits her periodically. He gives her a gift each time, but does not offer to maintain her in a regular way, which is what she would really like. Sometimes the gentleman reflects upon the fact that he has been the means of leading Moll into prostitution (as he thinks) and this bothers his conscience, but the thought wears off after a while, and he visits her again. After a time, however, he visits her less frequently and finally not at all. Moll must cast about for a way to make a living by her wits again.

One day she decides to wait at one of the inns where coaches leave London for the outlying towns. A servant-girl comes up in a great hurry to reserve a place on one of the coaches for her mistress, and Moll offers to "watch" her bundle for her. Of course, as soon as the girl's back is turned, Moll is off and soon loses herself among the London lanes. The package includes no money or silverware, but does contain some valuable clothes. The trick is repeated at various other inns, and successfully each time.

Comment

In the description of the scene at the coaching inn Defoe gives us another striking vignette of eighteenth-century life. His reproduction of casual conversation is especially interesting, as well as the bustle and confusion of catching the coach.

On another occasion Moll goes down to the docks and intercepts a young man who is trying to pick up some goods shipped to London from the North of England. She reads the letter which authorizes him to pick up the parcels. Then she sends him off, telling him that the warehouse is closed for the day, forges a copy of the letter and collects the merchandise herself.

Comment

When we reflect that Moll is supposed to have turned over a new leaf and to be deploring her past conduct, her tone here, and in fact all through the tale of her criminal career, is rather odd. She seems to take a great deal of pride in her skill and dexterity as a thief. Her obvious pleasure when she remembers past successes casts doubt in our minds on the sincerity of her repentance.

Moll's ability to read and write gave her a considerable advantage over her fellow thieves, most of whom were totally illiterate. Few members of the lower classes had either the time or the opportunity for education.

CHAPTER 10: A NARROW ESCAPE

As luck will have it, Moll is one day caught by the crowd which mistakes her for the similarly dressed culprit they are chasing. Brought back to the mercer's shop where the crime was committed, she protests her innocence, but one of the journeymen (paid apprentices) swears she is the right person. The mercer detains her in the shop by force, though she asks permission to call her friends and threatens to take legal action against him. The apprentices try to search her, but she resists. Just then the other shop assistants return, bringing the real criminal with them. The mercer now wants to release Moll, but she insists on going before a justice of the peace and bringing the mercer and the journeyman who first seized her. A great crowd has gathered, which is sympathetic to Moll; they throw things at the tradesman until he is forced to call a coach to protect himself, so Moll and her tormenter ride in style. The mercer is bound over to keep the peace and the journeyman is committed to Newgate Prison on a charge of assault.

When Moll arrives home her governess laughs heartily at the tale and seems very pleased. This annoys Moll, for she has hardly recovered from her fright, but the governess explains that she can sue the mercer for false arrest and probably collect a good sum. Moll is not sure about this course; what worries her is that she has had to give her name to the magistrate and she is afraid of becoming too well known in those circles.

An attorney is called and he advises that she bring suit immediately. A lively description of the law-suit follows. The mercer's representative tries to bribe Moll's lawyer to bring her to terms, but he honestly reports the attempt to Moll. For his part, he makes the mercer's party believe that Moll is a rich woman with important friends. At this they take fright and Moll's lawyer advises her that they are ready to settle out of court. Moll's attorney demands five hundred pounds and the other side offers fifty. A meeting is arranged, which Moll attends in elegant clothes and expensive jewelry, all stolen. The mercer is impressed and makes an elaborate apology, but Moll insists on damages as a matter of principle. They finally settle for one hundred fifty pounds, with the mercer to pay all the lawyer's fees. When she comes to collect the money, Moll arrives with her governess, "dressed like an old duchess," and a gentleman who is supposed to be her suitor. The journeyman is brought in and offers an abject apology, which Moll haughtily accepts.

MOLL FLANDERS

Comment

Here Defoe gives us one of the genuinely funny scenes in *Moll Flanders*. The picture of the two hardened criminals, Moll and her governess, dressed to the nines and graciously accepting the honest tradesman's submission, is an hilarious one. The detailed account of the conduct of an eighteenth-century lawsuit is also interesting. The abuses may be a little more blatant, but otherwise the incident does not seem very different from cases today. Defoe, of course, had a great deal of experience with the law, for as a merchant he was constantly suing and being sued. It was a litigious age, with everyone going to law on the slightest pretext. In Defoe's case, however, he was sued so many times for misrepresentation and business chicanery that his biographers (on the principle that you can't have smoke without a fire) have seriously suspected the honesty of his business dealings. In one case, in particular, he seems to have sold his mother-in-law a piece of property which he did not actually own!

CHAPTER 11: FURTHER ADVENTURES OF A NOTORIOUS THIEF

Having accumulated a fortune of seven hundred pounds, Moll counts herself the richest and most successful thief in England. She has had, she explains, "innumerable jobs besides those I have mentioned." Still she cannot resist trying her luck again. She goes out one evening dressed as a beggar and is given a gentleman's horse to hold outside a tavern. She steals the horse but then has no idea what to do with it! Her governess is as stymied as Moll; all they can think of is to take the horse to another inn and send the owner a note saying where it can be found, and they make nothing from the escapade. It is obvious that they must stick to the branch of the trade which they know; horse-stealing is a business for the experts in that specialty.

Comment

We are given a hint here that larceny has become an obsession with Moll. She even steals things she has no way of getting rid of! As Moll herself would express it, the devil has complete control of her.

She next falls in with a band of coiners, or as we would say, counterfeiters. She is still dressed as a beggar, and they offer her the job of working the press. She declines, for if they are caught, the penalties for forgery of this sort are extremely heavy. The person who is convicted of actually operating the press is burned at the stake and the thought fills Moll with horror. If she really were as poor as her dress makes her appear, she observes, she might be tempted to take the job, for those who starving have nothing to lose.

Comment

Remarks like this one, though they come from Moll's mouth, have their origin in Defoe's social consciousness. According to the thinking of the day, the only way to reduce crime was to apply still harsher penalties. As a result most offenses against property carried the death penalty, even when only a small sum was involved. With Moll as his spokesman, Defoe is pointing out here that even the most severe punishments are no deterrent to the destitute. They see their choice as the certainty of death by starvation as opposed to the chance of death on the gallows, and naturally choose the latter. In several of his works Defoe presents more humane ways of preventing crime.

An offer to join a party of housebreakers is also declined since Moll feels the risk is too great. A friend turns her attention to smuggled goods, but she is soon too well known among the smugglers and must give up further attempts. One day when she is passing the Exchange (the equivalent of our Stock Market) she sees a crowd gathering and hears that the queen is to pass that way.

Comment

At this time most important public buildings were lined with stalls selling all sorts of goods. They were even to be found in St. Paul's Cathedral and churchyard! The Exchange was no exception to this rule and since it was frequented by rich men, had some of the most expensive shops. Quick to take advantage of the confusion, she stands with her back to the counter of a milliner's shop and manages to filch a piece of lace while the shopkeeper is staring at the queen. Moll gets into a coach to avoid pursuit and just escapes the milliner's maids who are looking everywhere for her.

While walking in St. James' Park one day, Moll sees a girl of thirteen and her younger sister. The elder girl is wearing an expensive gold watch and pearl necklace. She goes up to the young ladies' footman, who is waiting for them to finish their walk, and engages him in conversation. (Footmen, who spent a good deal of time simply waiting around for their masters or mistresses, were notorious gossips.) Learning their names and something about them, she goes up to the girls and introduces herself as an old friend of the family. During their promenade she manages to lift the gold watch and then politely takes her leave without being suspected.

A rather different adventure presents itself when Moll decides to enter an expensive gambling house, a place where women were not usually seen. She pretends to be inexperienced and draws back from the tables, declaring that the stakes are too high for her.

Comment

Customs in gambling have changed very little since the eighteenth century and the modern dice-player will have no difficulty in following the game here. For those with less experience it should be explained that each player around the table has his turn with the dice and keeps throwing them until he "throws out" with an unlucky number (usually seven), the dice then passing to the next person.

At this, one of the gentlemen gives her ten guineas to bet for him. Moll has beginners luck, and after losing the first ten guineas is staked again and wins them back with a good deal more. She plays cautiously so as to keep a good pile of guineas in her lap and at every opportunity she hides a few of these in her pocket. At one point she has as much as eighty guineas, but loses her final throw and ends up with sixty-six. The man who staked her to begin with gives her half the winnings, so that, with what she has put away secretly for herself, she leaves the gambling house with seventy-three guineas, a very large sum. The governess advises her not to try her luck there again, for if she should be bitten with the gambling bug she would be sure to lose all she has. With this Moll agrees.

| Comment

We can see from this **episode** how different Moll is from the usual criminal. Since they are constantly gambling with their lives, they are almost drawn to gamble with their money as well. In this detail we can suspect that Defoe has made Moll like himself, as in many others. Although he took many business risks, Defoe was no gambler; gambling was considered a degrading vice by Dissenting middle-class people and Moll, like her creator, had middle-class instincts.

It is the quiet season in London, with few pickings for "the trade" as Moll calls it, and she joins a gang on a tour of the provincial fairs. They do not find the people as prosperous nor the means of escape as easy as in London, however, and booty is hard to come by. At Cambridge she has a package of cloth sent to her inn with the promise that she will pay for it later, and then sets off for the next town as soon as the delivery boy has left. This is an old trick, she says, which will pass in the provinces, but would not do for London.

At Harwich (the East Coast port from which boast left for Holland) she manages to take a Dutchman's large trunk out of the room next to hers at the inn, and a friendly porter carries it aboard the Ipswich wherry for her.

| Comment

Wherries were good-sized sailing vessels used for river traffic at this time in England. They were round-bottomed barge-like boats with a single large sail. There are still a few of them in use on the English rivers. Defoe describes the wherry and its use here in detail; it is just the kind of thing which he delighted in observing, and his guide book, *A Tour thro' the Whole Island of Great Britain*, as well as the better-known *Robinson Crusoe*, is full of just such descriptions.

She travels to Ipswich, where the customs inspectors open the trunk for her. Safely installed at an inn, she removes the valuables, including some French and Dutch money, and hires a horse to take her back to London. On the way she stops at Colchester, the scene of her girlhood, and inquires after the family which took care of her and her first lover. She never mentions, or seems to think of, her children.

Comment

Eventually we accept Moll's lack of concern about her offspring as a part of her character, brought about, no doubt, by the necessity she has been under of fending for herself all her life. Nevertheless, the complete absence of maternal feeling which she displays is somewhat repellent.

On her return to London she vows never to trust herself to the country again. She is a true child of London, and feels safe and happy only in its streets. At this juncture Moll, speaking from the vantage point of her old age, declares that each of her various adventures should serve as a warning for the reader, for similar traps are continually being laid for him. She adds that it is not for a person such as she is to draw the moral; the good reader must do that for himself.

Soon afterwards, on Christmas Day, she goes into a goldsmith's shop which is temporarily empty. She is just about to carry off a piece of silver plate when she is seized. Moll protests that she was looking about for the shopkeeper and had no intention of stealing anything. An alderman of the city, who is also a justice of the peace, happens to be passing and smooth things over, but not until he has made sure that Moll has the money to pay for what she insists she was trying to buy.

CHAPTER 12: CAUGHT AT LAST

Finally Moll trusts her luck too far and is caught with two pieces of silk brocade on her person; the serving-girls attack her as she is trying to escape. Though she pleads for mercy, the constable is sent for, she is taken before the magistrate and committed to Newgate Prison.

Comment

Newgate was for centuries the central London prison for those accused of civil crimes. Political prisoners, especially those of high rank, were usually sent to the Tower of London. According to all accounts, Newgate was a horrible place. Since so many crimes were punishable by death or transportation, there were few long-term prisoners except men jailed for debt. In any case, few prisoners survived the dampness, poor food and lack of exercise for long. Those who could afford to pay for better accommodations in Newgate got them, as Moll and her husband are able to do. The "joys" of Newgate are celebrated in that macabre but delightful eighteenth-century play, John Gay's *The Beggars' Opera*.

At last Moll's worst fears are realized. She has come full circle, back to the wretched place of her birth, and the only deliverance she can hope for is death. Her former accomplices and those who have envied the success of her criminal career gloat over her. She finds her fellow prisoners resigned to their fate but Moll herself is cast into despair. Her old governess does all she can, attempting to bribe the witnesses and buy off the merchant, but without success.

Moll's case does not come up at the first court session, and as time passes she becomes inured even to the terrors or prison. In retrospect she calls this a kind of madness and says that her nature itself must be degenerate to enable her to put up with these conditions.

Comment

Defoe does not try to make excuses for Moll's crimes, but he does try to point out the good things in her character. Two of the virtues which he emphasizes constantly are her courage and adaptability. Both are fully displayed during her stay in Newgate.

In spite of her hopeless situation, Moll has neither remorse nor true repentance. She can only dwell on the horrors of death and damnation; she says that "a certain strange lethargy of soul possessed me." She is roused for a little by the appearance of her Lancashire husband, Jemmie, who has been captured as a highwayman. Soon afterward the grand jury brings in an indictment and Moll is remanded for trial. One of the keepers comes to her and bids her settle her affairs with God, for the case is very black against her. The governess seems more repentant than Moll is, though she is in no danger.

The trial is over all too soon. The serving wenches who are witnesses make the worst of the case against Moll, saying that she had the cloth under her clothes and was going out the door when they stopped her. She, for her part, says that she was only taking it out to look at it in better light. Unfortunately for her, the house in which she was taken is that of a broker, and not of a retail merchant, so this argument holds very little water. She is allowed to speak before sentence is passed, and makes an eloquent plea for mercy, but in spite of this she is found guilty and sentenced to death.

The governess is so affected by this turn of events that she sends for a minister and resolves to begin a new life; Moll adds from her vantage point in time that the woman really did give up her criminal career and continued repentant until the day of her death.

Comment

To the modern reader, evangelistic statements of this sort sound crude and rather funny, but Defoe's audience read the book in part for just this kind of moral-drawing. In this portion of *Moll Flanders* especially, Defoe is more preacher than novelist.

Moll's friend also sends a minister to her and under his guidance and the horror of imminent death, our heroine begins to set her spiritual house in order and to experience true contrition. The thought of the delights of heaven makes her realize how stupid she has been to forfeit it for silly and transient earthly pleasure. Although she maintains that, "I am not capable of reading lectures of instruction to anybody, ..." she goes on for a good while in this vein. She confesses to the minister the terrible tale of her past life.

The warrant for Moll's execution arrives, but the afternoon before the scheduled hanging the minister obtains a reprieve. At this point Moll says, in an aside to her audience, that although the people who read the book for a sensational story of crime may be bored with the part about her repentance, this part is the best and most instructive section of the book.

The execution of the other condemned prisoners is a severe shock to Moll, who breaks down and cries hysterically. Then her mood reverses itself; she is moved by gratitude and joy, and is even more pleased when her petition to be transported to the Colonies instead of executed is granted. Moll's governess, who has just recovered from a serious illness, now visits her and together they try to arrange things to make Moll's life as a transported convict as easy as possible. As her governess cheerfully points out, she has money, which is the one indispensable thing, and more than most convicts have.

CHAPTER 13: THE RETURN OF THE HIGHWAYMAN

After a delay of nearly four months, Moll is put on board a ship in the River Thames with thirteen other criminals. She mentions that these thirteen were the most hardened and audacious villains in all Newgate in her time, and it would take a book longer than her own to describe their misdeeds. However, she has a very interesting account of all their lives and in particular of their behavior on the voyage, which the captain of the ship on which they traveled arranged to have written down.

Comment

In having Moll make this obviously unbelievable statement, Defoe betrays himself as the journalist and serial writer. It was a method of self-advertisement, a way of saying, "Look for the wonderful adventures of-which I am going to publish next year!" In this way he could test public reaction to his proposal and see if it would be worthwhile to write a book on this subject. *Robinson Crusoe* contains a number of "feelers" of this sort, and of course he did write a continuation of that.

Moll now reverts back in time to her stay in prison and returns to the subject of her Lancashire husband, whom she saw brought into Newgate.

Comment

The occasional disruption of chronological order is one of the most confusing features of Defoe's style. We unconsciously assign it to Moll's rambling style of reminiscence, but it is still a flaw in the work.

He is kept in prison for several months, for the authorities lack sufficient evidence against him but hope that in time more witnesses will appear. Notices are posted that anyone who has been robbed and thinks he can identify the men should come forward. Moll takes this opportunity of taking a look at her husband, but she disguises herself so thoroughly that he does not recognize her. The prison grapevine carries the rumor that the notorious Moll Flanders is going to turn state's evidence against the highwayman and Jemmie asks to see his accuser. When they are alone together Moll identifies herself and her husband is overcome with astonishment. When he recovers he reproaches her for making a mockery of him by coming to visit him in jail, but she interrupts to say that her condition is worse than his. The news that she is not only a prisoner in the same jail, but has already been convicted and sentenced to death, makes him speechless. She gives him a rather colored and favorable account of her career since they parted and says that most of her troubles stem from being mistaken for the infamous Moll Flanders and thus treated as an old offender.

Comment

It is typical of Moll to tell less than the whole truth, even to someone she loves. This defensive behavior has been taught her by hard experience; she has little enough reason to trust anyone, and the long period she has spent in the company of other thieves has made her doubly careful. Preserving her privacy at all costs, however, is also part of her basic outlook on life. She has a strong feeling of alienation; that is, she is convinced that she is utterly alone and must struggle single-handed against the rest of the world. When viewed in this light, her behavior becomes quite understandable.

Continuing their reminiscences, Moll tells the highwayman how she spoke up and thus threw the mob off his track years ago, just outside London. He smiles at this and tells her that she saved his life, for that was the only time in his career of robbery until the present that he was in mortal danger. He now tells Moll the history of his life which, she comments, ".... would make a very strange history, and be infinitely diverting." He "took to the road" (that is, became a highwayman) about twelve years before he met her. The woman who introduced Moll to him was not his sister but an accomplice of the gang of highwaymen, who gave them information when rich travelers were leaving town. He also mentions that had Moll been an heiress, as he thought she was, he would have retired from his criminal career (on her money) and become a respectable citizen. On several occasions he made such large hauls that he would have been ready to give up "the trade" and to accept Moll's earlier proposal of emigrating to Virginia, if only he had known where to find her. Various adventures are related, including one in which he rides eighty miles with his arm shattered by a pistol bullet before daring to seek medical attention.

Comment

Accounts of the lives of highwaymen (and pirates) were one of the most popular forms of literature for the lower classes. What Defoe has done here is to adapt incidents from several such stories, some of them true and some traditional in the "annals of the road." The traditional bravery and resourcefulness of highwaymen made their careers particularly glamorous, rather like those of international espionage agents in modern fiction. One of the most famous highwaymen of literature is Macheath in John Gay's *Beggars' Opera*. Readers of today may be more familiar with him as Mack the Knife in Bertolt Brecht's modern adaptation of Gay's musical play, *The Threepenny Opera*.

Moll breaks off her relation of Jemmie's career "with great reluctance," but as she observes, this is her story, not his. Upon inquiring into Jemmie's legal situation, his wife finds that there is only scanty evidence against him, though more may turn up. He has heard that the authorities would be willing to dispense with a trial if he would consent to have himself transported, but he feels that he would rather be hanged than accept this alternative. Moll upbraids him for speaking in this way and points out that once he is overseas and free of criminal prosecution, there are many ways of getting back to England again. She adds that if he accepts this way out, there may even be some means of avoiding transportation altogether.

Jemmie tells her that his mind rebels at being sent to work on the plantations like a slave, and that most of his profession agree with him that the hangman's noose is at least the end of all the troubles of this world, whatever the next may offer. Moll uses every argument she can think of to change his mind, including tears. She also points out that for those with some money, transportation is not slavery; for a reasonable sum, everything can be "arranged." Her husband points out, rather unfairly, that Moll herself would not be so eager to be transported if she did not already know the country and have close relatives there besides. To this Moll retorts that her mother must have died long since and that she be would very unwilling to identify herself to her other relations, with whom she has lost contact. She guarantees that under her management he will the certainty of living have like a gentleman in America, especially since he has hinted that he has money.

Comment

By this time we should not be surprised to hear Moll say that money is "the only friend," in spite of her very recent resolution to change the whole course of her life. Her middle-class outlook, which makes money the touchstone of everything, is so deeply engrained in her character that there is no possibility of changing it. From all we can gather of Defoe's life, this attitude toward money was one that he shared with his heroine.

At this Jemmie bridles and denies he has ever said he has money. Quickly Moll reassures him that she is not looking for money from him, but on the contrary might be able to help him on that score. Then he relents and shows himself willing to share what little he has with his wife.

Comment

Moll and her husband are so much two of a kind on this score that the result is very amusing. In spite of all their past and future protestations of undying love, and the pleasant shock of their unexpected reunion, as soon as the subject of money arises, they become like two fencers circling warily around one another, each one desperately on the defensive. It is one of the ironic features of the book that it is money which first separates Moll and her highwayman lover (or rather the lack of it) and it is also money, the necessity to pool their resources, which finally brings them together.

Jemmie is finally persuaded to ask to be transported and he and Moll take an affectionate leave of each other. Once he has applied Moll realizes that her own last-minute efforts to obtain a full pardon must end unless she wants to abandon her husband and let him be transported alone, a thing he refuses to do. However, she conceals this fact from the minister who "converted" her and had her sentence commuted; he has been working hard to have her remain in the country and thus under his spiritual direction. She does not want to hurt his feelings.

After her extended flash-back, Moll now returns us to the ship anchored in the Thames. The ship drops down to the mouth of the river and anchors again to prevent any chance of escape. She has the ship's boatswain take a letter to her governess informing her of her whereabouts, and takes the opportunity to let the sailor see that she is well provided with money. She has the governess send her what she needs, but she is careful not to have supplies consigned under her own name because she is a prisoner. Everything necessary to make her comfortable on the ship is provided, although she takes care that nothing is so luxurious that it arouses the envy of her companions. At the same time she is careful to leave part of her money with the governess for future contingencies. A letter from Jemmie informs her that he is unlikely to be allowed to join her ship, for the formalities are not yet completed. He is very distressed at this possibility. The governess sets herself to get him released in time; she succeeds and also arranges that he will not be classed as a convicted felon with the others because of course he is not. He and Moll are finally reunited, but she finds him very dejected at the thought of leaving England.

Comment

Moll puts a great deal of stress on her husband's inability to take care of himself and his lack of fortitude; she feels the need to dominate her husbands and, in the main, does so very successfully. Courage is one of Moll's outstanding virtues; it is not surprising that she considers the lack of it in others a sign of weakness.

A kind of audit is now taken of their joint wealth; Jemmie has only 108 pounds left after the expenses of his prison stay and the necessary bribes, and Moll has 246 pounds and a few shillings with her; the money she has left in reserve with the governess she does not mention, even to him. Together, Moll computes, they have 354 pounds, and she remarks that it is an estate obtained by worse means than any in England. The thought does not seem to bother her much. The only thing that upsets her is that it is all in money, whereas if they could take the same sum in goods to the Colonies, they could reap a good profit.

Comment

Moll's incurably mercantile character comes to the fore again. After a near escape from hanging and reunion with a beloved husband, with the prospect of starting a new life in America before her, she is still irked by the thought of losing a quick and easy profit.

In addition, Moll has in her chest two gold watches, some pieces of silver plate and some rings, all stolen during her previous career. She sums up her position by saying (and her resolution is nowhere seen more clearly), "... and in the sixty-first year of my age, I launched out into a new world, ..."

With a little money bestowed in the right places, our heroine and her husband are given a private cabin like the other non-convict passengers and arrange to eat at the first mate's table. To top everything off, the governess ingratiates herself with the captain to such an extent that they get their stock of goods shipped on board after all, including a large supply of tools and even furniture! The complaisant captain permits them to take a last trip ashore; they order a good dinner at an inn, stay all night and return with a few extra little luxuries for the voyage, including ten dozen bottles of beer.

Comment

The capacity to make the best of a difficult situation is an ability which Defoe very much admires. The accumulation of tools, the gradual progression from necessities to luxuries, is a process which he enjoys describing; the same kind of situation can be seen in most of his novels, but the most elaborate example of "making-do," of course, is in *Robinson Crusoe*. The gradual production of comfort by one's own unaided efforts is a perennially attractive **theme** which readers never fail to enjoy. Books as dissimilar as *Swiss Family Robinson* and our own pioneer sagas have utilized it.

The ship sets sail, and after experiencing contrary winds, finally arrives in Virginia. Here Moll and her husband are "sold" as servants to a planter, in accordance with the terms of their transportation. A financial arrangement with their friend the captain of the ship, however, insures that this sale is only a formality, and after a convivial bowl of rum punch in a tavern they are free to go where they will.

Comment

Defoe seems inconsistent here, for Jemmy has gone to the Colonies voluntarily and thus should not be sold as a convict.

CHAPTER 14: IN WHICH MOLL'S ADVENTURES END HAPPILY

The new settlers get their cargo off the ship and then Moll inquires after her mother and half-brother. Her mother is dead, but her brother (also her ex-husband, as Moll reminds us) is alive, which is disturbing news to Moll. Still more disturbing is the information that he and one of his sons have moved and are now living close by the Potomac, where the ship has docked. Moll reflects, however, that after this interval it would be impossible for anyone to recognize her. She is curious to see him, and approaching his plantation she observes him at a little distance with her own son, Humphrey. Moll muffles her face as they pass, though as it turns out there is no need of this, for her old husband is nearly blind. It is a wrench for Moll to see her son, a handsome and prosperous-looking young man, and not be able to make herself known to him. When they have passed, Moll pretends that she feels unwell and lying down on the ground, weeps and kisses the place over which he had walked.

Comment

It seems rather extraordinary that this is almost the first time in the book that Moll has expressed concern or emotion over any of her children. Moll, however, is sentimental when practical considerations are not involved; perhaps it would be cynical to suggest that what affects her is the sight of a prosperous son who may be of great help to his newly-arrived and (relatively) destitute mother.

As Moll is returning with her companion, a woman of the neighborhood, the woman tells her a strange piece of local gossip concerning the old man. It seems that he married a fine woman but she eventually learned he was her half-brother and went away. Moll is both moved and disturbed to hear her own story recited in this way.

Comment

This ingenuous repetition of a flattering description of herself fits in perfectly with the picture we have already formed of

Moll's character. She thinks very well of herself and probably feels that the woman's remarks are no more than just.

The heroine soon recovers enough to ask some questions about her mother: how she died and more particularly, about the details of her will. The woman tells her that a sum of money has been left for the daughter (Moll) if she should ever be heard of again. This is the news Moll has been waiting to hear.

How to make herself known to her son and collect the money, or whether she should do it at all, is now the question that torments Moll. She is so obviously distracted that Jemmie insists on knowing what is wrong, but she puts him off by making up a story based largely on the facts.

She contemplates moving to another colony, but reflects that then she would have to give up her inheritance. At the same time, she cannot bring herself to tell her present husband about her earlier (and still legally valid) incestuous marriage. The memory of her tormented state of mind at this time makes Moll observe that everyone should have a confidant for their secrets; it is not natural to keep them entirely to oneself. She says wisely that this is why so many otherwise discreet people have betrayed themselves; secrets, by their very nature, will find an outlet, and she proceeds to give examples.

Comment

Critics have found this kind of digression one of the most serious flaws in Defoe's fiction. Moll has arrived at a crisis of some seriousness, but instead of prolonging or heightening the tension, the author goes off into psychological speculation. That he knows it is a digression is plain enough; he has Moll give a kind of apology for it. Since the book is published for its moral, she says, the reader should realize the importance of the problem she is discussing. Despite her claim, however, this aside on secrets is obviously irrelevant.

Returning to her **theme**, Moll decides that they should move to another colony and gets her husband to agree. They settle on Carolina, because of its warm climate, but still the thought of her son and her inheritance preys on Moll's mind. She considers sending her husband on ahead to Carolina, but realizes that he will not leave her and besides has neither knowledge of the country nor the ability to choose and establish a plantation.

At last Moll determines to move to Carolina where they will not be known, and then return to claim her legacy. In this way she can avoid being identified as a transported convict. They have a bad trip down the river and across the bay to Maryland and decide to settle there, having had enough of traveling. They meet an honest Quaker who directs them to a fertile piece of land and helps them in many ways.

Comment

The trip down the Potomac River and across Chesapeake Bay provides Defoe with an opportunity to show off his geographical knowledge. His interest in world trade had made him very knowledgeable on this subject, and he published his *Atlas Maritimus & Commercialis* in 1728. Clearly, among the attractions of books of adventure like *Moll Flanders* for the reader were the descriptions of foreign lands.

One of their first acts is to buy two servants, one an Englishwoman just arrived from Liverpool, and the other a negro manservant. They soon have fifty acres cleared and part of it planted in tobacco.

Comment

Presumably the Englishwoman is a bondservant and the Negro a slave, but Moll makes no distinction between them. The **irony** of the fact that she and her husband have themselves only barely escaped from just such bondslavery, and the horror with which she regarded such a fate for herself, apparently does not even cross their minds.

Now that their own plantation is started, Moll returns to the estate of her husband-brother. She writes him a letter which is designed to allay his fears and puts in a claim for her portion of her mother's estate. In the letter she is careful to include many tender expressions regarding her son and the longing she feels as a mother to see him again; she has calculated that her brother, with his bad sight, will be certain to ask their son to read the letter to him. Things fall out better than she could have hoped, for the son rides straight back with the messenger who brought the letter and greets his mother warmly. Moll is overjoyed at seeing her son again, and even more enraptured to hear that the disposal of his grandmother's estate is in his hands.

Moll's reception is so cordial, and her son's offers to look after her so obviously sincere, that she begins to regret having brought Jemmie along with her from England. The income from the plantation which has been left to Moll by her mother comes to one hundred pounds a year, which the son undertakes to pay on the spot. This good fortune, equally unexpected and unfamiliar, moves Moll to thank Providence, and she adds that she never felt such remorse for her past life as now when the

Fates are smiling on her. Moll promises to make the son her heir, since he is the only child whose whereabouts she knows, and presents him with one of her (stolen) gold watches.

When she returns to Maryland she brings back livestock, farm equipment and all sorts of other presents from her dutiful son. She displays her treasures to Jemmie, who exclaims over God's unexpected mercies to one so unworthy as he is. Moll adds for him that thereafter his penitence was as sincere as anyone could wish. The plantation flourishes and Jemmie is at last able to realize his life-long ambition of living like a gentleman. Moll has her friend the governess invest her remaining money in goods to be shipped to America, including fine swords, guns and harnesses for her husband. After reckoning up their wealth, and all the things Moll has brought him, Jemmie bursts out that despite what he thought after he first married her in Lancashire, she was an heiress after all.

On her second visit to her son to collect the year's income, Moll hears to her relief that her half-brother has died. She now tells Jemmie the whole story of her incestuous marriage; after a decent interval she tells her son that she is thinking of marrying, and then that she is married. The son visits them and presumably delights in his future inheritance. At the time of writing, Moll concludes, she is seventy years old. She and Jemmie have returned to England in prosperity, and intend to spend the remainder of their lives in penitence for their past misdeeds.

Comment

It is hard to believe that Moll is not being cynical during this last part of her memoirs, but according to the critics and everything we know of Defoe's life, that is what we must believe. She is so single-mindedly and unconsciously selfish that she does not even seem to be aware of the subconscious connection between the delight at seeing her son and the fact that he can give her large presents in land and money. In the same way, Jemmie's "true repentance" occurs only after he has seen the very tangible rewards of their new life. According to Puritan beliefs, God may use any kind of key to unlock the hearts of sinners. For Moll and her husband, the key is a golden one; they are bribed to repent.

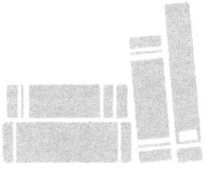

MOLL FLANDERS

CHARACTER ANALYSES

MOLL FLANDERS

In any analysis of the characters of *Moll Flanders* we must bear in mind Defoe's statement that he is writing a "true history," that is, a genuine autobiography. He intends the reader to derive a moral lesson from the book at the same time. It is designed, the author says, as a deterrent to crime and as an example of the fruits of repentance. Defoe, it seems, meant the moral aspect of the novel to be taken perfectly seriously, though to modern eyes it teaches a strange kind of morality. Since the book purports to be autobiographical, we should not be surprised to find that Moll is the main character, and that all other figures are completely subordinate. In most cases they are not even given names. This lack of names supports the feeling of **realism**, for most of Moll's associates are on the run from the law; until we try to take the book apart critically, we hardly notice the omission. The minor figures are no more than a supporting cast, little more than "props," in fact for, Moll herself.

MOLL'S REAL IDENTITY IS CONCEALED

Moll tells us that she cannot use her real name because it is too well known to the London criminal courts (the Old Bailey) and in Newgate Prison. The statement is typical of the confusion produced by Defoe's rapid journalistic style of writing and his carelessness about details. For the heroine is just as well known at Newgate by the name of Moll Flanders as under her "real" name. In addition, she is supposed to be writing the book upon her return to England in her old age. In that case she cannot use either her "real" name or that of Moll Flanders because they are both too well known to the police. We also presume that she has taken the name of her "Lancashire husband" in the ordinary way and thus there is no reason for her to use her old names. The explanation she gives is both unnecessary and misleading, but it serves Defoe's intention. It gives the reader notice that this will be a rogue biography, one of the accounts of criminal lives that were so popular among lower and middle-class readers in the early eighteenth century.

MOLL'S MORAL CHARACTER

The fact that Defoe models his work on the rogue biographies brings us to the question which impresses us most forcefully as we read *Moll Flanders*. Is Moll essentially criminal; that is to say, does she have the "criminal mind"? The only fair answer to this question, if we have followed the heroine's actions carefully and listened to her statements, is an emphatic "No!" The author is extremely careful to show her as the product of circumstances, the victim of a succession of unlucky chances. Moll's moral fiber is not very strong, but we are given every reason to suppose that had one or other of her husbands survived, she would have ended her days as a contented housewife in Colchester or a tradesman's wife in London. In the main, the heroine's illegal and immoral actions are forced upon her by the necessity for survival. Here we see Defoe's social consciousness at work. As a bankrupt and debtor pursued by the bailiffs at various times in his life, he was very much aware of the depressed class in eighteenth-century England which faced the alternatives of crime or starvation.

MIDDLE-CLASS MORALITY

If Moll Flanders does not have a criminal mind, it is fair to ask what class her ideas do reflect. In the answer we see some of Defoe's own strengths and weaknesses as a novelist. In her thinking, if not in her financial position, Moll is unmistakably a member of the middle class. Her ideas reflect Defoe's; within reasonable limits we can say that Defoe made her mind like his own, just as he made *Robinson Crusoe's*. This middle-class philosophy, or tradesman's mentality, can be seen in Moll's tendency to view every event in terms of a financial transaction. When she talks of selling her virtue she means the phrase quite literally. It is a commodity to be auctioned off to the highest bidder. Her formal religious thinking (what there is of it) is also like Defoe's. The author was a Dissenter, that is, a member of a rather fundamentalist Protestant group, and we see Moll acting as a Dissenter when she insists on drawing a moral lesson from everything she does. Here we must go along with Defoe's ideas if the story is not to seem hopelessly contradictory. The heroine is supposed to be looking back on her misspent past with repentance, and pointing out the moral of her wayward life to her readers. The fact that she relates her escapades with such gusto and dwells with obvious pleasure on the physical charms of her youth is simply a case of Defoe writing effectively in spite of himself. It has nothing to do with the supposed moral. We must accept this enthusiasm as part of Moll's character (and a rather ingratiating part to the modern reader); she can glory in her past and repent of it at the same time.

THE MIDDLE-CLASS ETHOS

In *Moll Flanders* we see at work the new ethical ideas which are associated with the rise to power of the middle class. The new morality of the Puritans or Dissenters (for our purpose the terms can be used interchangeably) is expressed in relative terms, as compared with the absolute moral standards of earlier Protestantism. Dissenters, like Defoe, looked for direct action from their God. They equated business success with moral righteousness, and failure with immorality. We see Moll Flanders reflecting this same attitude. For her, failure in business, poverty, is the ultimate evil, and anything which acts to stave off poverty can be condoned. By extension, any affair which terminates successfully must have at least the tacit approval of the Deity. The time scheme of the novel adds to confusion here. It is hard to disentangle Moll's emotions at the time the action takes place from her reflections at the time of writing. But whether in the middle of her life or at the end of it, what Moll seems to repent most sincerely is not doing wrong but getting caught at it. The shallowness of the morality which Moll exhibits is one of the most striking features of the book; it is amusing that the lack of depth does not seem in the least apparent to the author. Typical of her attitude are her remarks about the crime of incest. The tenor of her remarks is: "If only we had not found out that we were brother and sister, everything would have been all right!" The intense practicality of this moral code is part of what makes *Moll Flanders* so different from earlier books. Previous authors had stuck close to an ideal moral code; Defoe showed morality as it really was among the middle class. This disenchanted view of human nature is one of the components of Defoe's **realism**. According to natural law as it was interpreted by the eighteenth-century bourgeoisie, the individual owed it to himself to be as successful as possible. It is this morality of exploitation which typifies *Moll Flanders*.

WHY MOLL IS A "MODERN" CHARACTER

Another facet of Moll's character which seems distinctively modern to us is her sense of individualism, her feeling that she is an isolated entity. She sees life as a struggle between herself and the world, and the struggle is for survival. Moll sees life in these terms even though she still gives lip service to the Puritan religion, which advocated direct reliance on God. The eighteenth century saw a greatly increased interest in the principles of "natural law": that law which an individual could find within himself, as opposed to the law of society (the law enforced by the police and the courts) or even Divine law. Moll reduces natural law to its lowest common denominator, the law of self-preservation. Unconsciously, and sometimes consciously as well, she feels that any course is justified which will keep her alive. In actual fact, of course, she is never reduced to a level even approaching starvation; she constantly exaggerates the seriousness of her position. But the danger to Defoe and his readers must have seemed real enough in an England filled with beggars and a London seething with slumdwellers. The author knew Newgate Prison only too well, and Newgate was full of those who, like Moll herself, risked the horrors of prison, transportation, and the gallows in order to steal enough to stay alive. Defoe is not exaggerating the law at all when he has

Moll's mother transported for stealing three pieces of holland (linen cloth), or when Moll's own death sentence, commuted to transportation, results from stealing two pieces of silk brocade. Such savagery was felt by the law-makers to be the only possible deterrent to the almost overwhelming temptation to steal.

MOLL'S RELATIONSHIPS WITH OTHERS

The extreme sense of individualism which Moll illustrates can be seen very clearly in her relationships with the other characters in the novel. Her first thought is always for herself and her own interest. No matter how much she protests that she loves someone, she is always careful not to forfeit her economic independence. The greater part of her stock of money or goods she keeps to herself. This attitude on Moll's part adds to the **realism** of the book. She has learned through bitter experience that no one else will look out for her if she does not look out for herself. But what we find most striking is that she sees no contradiction between her expressions for love of others and her overwhelmingly selfish actions. We feel that she is either being very naive or ironic. The first choice seems to be the true one. She has the protective naivete of complete individualism. As Ian Watt puts it in his brilliant book, *The Rise of the Novel*, " .... for Defoe and his heroine, generous sentiments are good, and concealed cash reserves are good too, perhaps better; but there is no feeling that they conflict, or that one attitude undermines the other." Here again we can see how Defoe has made Moll Flanders like himself; he seems as unaware as his heroine of the ironic implications of what he is writing. He maintains that he has edited Moll's story and presents it as a tract against wickedness, but the moral lesson of the book is of the most superficial kind. To modern readers, the moral could easily be: "Don't repent until you have built up an adequate income through crime." Moll herself is not punished in any effective way, and does not retire from her criminal career until advancing age and a desire for security outweigh her love of money. She uses others so single-mindedly that the subordinate characters appear hardly more than her tools or means to an end. As a result of this emphasis, there is no need to characterize them carefully or make them strongly individualized; we are only interested in these lesser figures as they affect Moll.

MOLL'S PERSONALITY

To sum up the personality of Moll Flanders, we can see that she is ambitious and motivated by pride. Even as a little girl she wishes to be a "gentlewoman," a station far above that to which she is born. Her strong individualism takes the form of an almost complete selfishness. She is clever at judging those around her, and understands human nature very well, but the knowledge is utilized almost entirely to enable Moll to make use of others. At the same time her individualism takes more attractive forms. She is self-reliant and full of a dogged courage. Defoe apparently felt this persistent courage against odds was a characteristic of the English lower classes, and was lacking in the more finely bred aristocrats. Moll's basic instinct is for survival, and survive she does, against all the forces that try to sweep her under. If we take into account only these characteristics, Moll seems like a grim sort of person, but she is not. She is able to see the humor or **irony** of life, sometimes in her own misfortunes and always in those of others. She is incurably optimistic, always convinced that her next trip, her next adventure, her next husband will bring her the security she longs for. Passion and sentiment are both apparent in her character. The scenes of separation from and reunion with the husbands she really loves, particularly Jemmie, the Lancashire highwayman, are genuinely affecting and contrast strongly with the occasions when she is displaying the more calculating side of her nature. The contradictions in Moll's character make her seem more human and more interesting to the reader. She longs for security but cannot stop stealing even when she has enough money to live on for years. She declares her love in passionate terms but is careful to preserve part of her fortune intact in case of emergencies. These conflicts have been pointed out as examples of Defoe's carelessness and inconsistency, but the fact that Moll does not know her own mind really only makes her one of us. She is "modern," in part, because she is in no sense a type but a living person.

MOLL'S MOTHER

In accordance with eighteenth-century ideas of heredity, Defoe makes Moll Flander's mother very much like Moll herself. She is a convicted criminal, and it is only because she is going to have a child that she escapes the gallows. Like Moll, she talks as if she were sentimental but is really very practical. When she finds out that her son and daughter have been living together as man and wife, she suggests that the fact be concealed from the son - that Moll and her husband should continue as before! The character of her mother gives one of the rare clues as to why Moll is the kind of person she is.

MOLL'S NURSE

The woman who takes Moll into her home and rears and instructs her until she is fourteen years old is an example of the simple, good countrywoman who appears frequently in eighteenth-century fiction. Though she tries to set Moll's feet on the right path, there is already something in the girl's character that will eventually lead her astray. Defoe inserts the portrait of the nurse to show that Moll did not always lack guidance.

THE COLCHESTER FAMILY

The family that takes Moll in as a kind of companion to their daughters is typical of the country gentry of Defoe's time. This class formed the backbone of the Tory party and the Established Church. Defoe, whose politics and religion were opposed to theirs, may have deliberately set out to show that their behavior was not always in accordance with their principles. The elder brother who first seduces Moll is interested exclusively in his own pleasure, despite his protestations of love. His sisters are fond of Moll only until her beauty and talents threaten to outshine theirs. The mother is amiable but obviously unable to control her children or safeguard the moral climate of her home, while the father is so involved in business that he has no time for his offspring.

MOLL'S FIRST HUSBAND

The exception in this self-centered family is the younger brother, Master Robert, or Robin as he is usually called. His love for Moll is perfectly honorable, and he chooses her in the face of considerable opposition from his parents and sisters, who object to his marrying a penniless girl. We must remember that Defoe is writing the sensational history of a sinful life, not a diary of domesticity, and thus Moll's five years of presumably happy married life with Robert, as well as the birth of two children, are passed over in a single line. Moll has no compulsion to criminal activity, and we can assume that if her husband had not died she would have remained a faithful wife and mother to the end of her days. (In that case, of course, there would be no story.) The role of chance in shaping mens' destinies always intrigued Defoe.

MOLL'S SECOND HUSBAND

The author's sense of social propriety, his feeling that the middle class should not try to ape the manners of their betters, is reflected in his description of the heroine's next consort: "... this amphibious creature, this land-water thing called a gentleman-tradesman;". He wastes his money and Moll's own. (Even at her most frivolous, Moll reckons up, typically, that a pleasure trip to Oxford and Northampton cost precisely 93 pounds.) Within a short space of time he is bankrupt, escapes arrest for debt by fleeing to France, and Moll never sees him again.

MOLL'S THIRD HUSBAND

After this experience our heroine has learned the value of economy and a rich husband and deliberately sets out to find one. The man she finds deceives her about his wealth, just as she deceives him about her own. When their mutual poverty is discovered they go to Virginia. There Moll discovers her mother and the fact that she is married to her half brother. Defoe makes the contrast between the reactions of Moll and of her husband to the discovery very marked. In her tough-minded way, Moll is quickly able to dismiss the matter from her consciousness, but her half brother is overwhelmed by the news. He faints away, soon afterward attempts suicide unsuccessfully, and contracts a lingering illness. Moll's attitude towards this weakness is demonstrated by her remark near the end of the book: "... when the old wretch my brother was dead...."

MOLL'S CHILDREN

One of the least attractive aspects of Moll's self-absorption is her lack of maternal feeling. Although she gives birth to about ten children, and occasionally expresses concern about whether or not they are "provided for," she seems to forget them as soon as they are out of her sight. It is ironic (though will Defoe it is difficult to tell whether the **irony** is intentional) that the one child about whom Moll does express tender feelings is her son by her half brother, and this child is in a position to give his mother a substantial fortune. None of the other children is described in any detail.

THE GENTLEMAN AT BATH

The affair with the married man whom Moll meets at Bath gives Defoe an occasion for a little homily on the danger of taking too much pride in one's virtue and tempting it too far. The gentleman is typical of the minor characters in *Moll Flanders*. We have little idea of his appearance or his nature, and his actions are rather wooden and highly predictable. It is in this kind of characterization that the crudeness of the author's technique (typical of early attempts in a new form such as the novel) can be seen. Moll takes the first steps towards seducing the man, and thus when he is frightened by illness into turning over a new leaf and abandons her, she has no one to blame but herself.

THE BANK CLERK (MOLL'S FIFTH HUSBAND)

The bank clerk is another of these minor characters. (There were very few books in Defoe's time in which the heroine's husband is a minor character.) He is not described with much care, but Defoe's gift for realistic detail is sometimes effective in spite of himself. The clerk's mixture of meticulous propriety and passion are highly amusing. He rushes Moll into marriage, but not until he has shown her the legal proof of divorce from his previous wife, her death certificate, and the verdict of the coroner's jury.

THE LANCASHIRE HUSBAND (MOLL'S FOURTH)

James E., or Jemmie, as Moll calls him, is one of the few figures who attains any stature in comparison with Moll herself. He appeals to Moll's romantic nature, which is never entirely suppressed by her more practical side. As a gentleman of fortune (the expression means one who is looking for a fortune, not a man who has one already) and a highwayman, he has the qualities of courage and unscrupulous determination which she admires. For Jemmie, Moll seems to have a genuine passion; the scenes of their separations and reunions are affecting because they have the ring of sincerity. Yet in the long run Jemmie's courage is not equal to Moll's own. She has to persuade him, much against his will, to take the frightening option of transportation to the colony of Virginia rather than the chance of being hanged. The preoccupation of Moll's husband with tangible rewards, and the shallowness of his religious ideas (which match Moll's own) can be seen by his remark once they are settled comfortably in the Colonies. They are far more prosperous than he could have hoped, and when he sees the golden evidence of this fact with his own eyes he bursts out, "What is God a-doing for such an ungrateful dog as I am!" Moll adds for him, "... and from this time forward I believe he was as sincere a penitent, and as thoroughly a reformed man, as ever God's goodness brought back from a profligate, a highwayman, and a robber." Here again the cynical have seen Defoe's moral as, "Repent! ... once you have the cash in hand."

THE MIDWIFE

The midwife who takes care of Moll while she has Jemmie's child, and afterwards becomes her tutor and partner in crime, is almost a mirror image of Moll herself. She is exceedingly businesslike about her illegal activities, with a graduated scale of charges for unmarried mothers, and a nice sense of the market value of stolen goods. She has the traditional loyalty of thieves and does everything she can for Moll when the heroine is in Newgate Prison. A curious fact about the personal relationships of the characters in *Moll Flanders* can be seen here. The story is, of course, told by Moll, and everything is seen through her eyes. In view of this, it is a curious coincidence that everyone with whom Moll comes in contact for any length of time, male or female, is inspired by an overwhelming devotion to her, even though for the most part they are the most abandoned criminals.

Since the heroine is telling her own story we must allow her license here, but we wonder if all these people are really so devoted to Moll, or if this is merely one of her many delusions. In any case, the midwife is perhaps the most interesting member of Defoe's gallery of underworld creatures.

VARIOUS MINOR CHARACTERS

The numerous still more minor characters whom Defoe introduces in various **episodes** serve, as far as the mechanics of the story are concerned, to advance the plot and act as confederates or victims for Moll herself. At the same time, and perhaps without being fully aware of it, Defoe has provided a fascinating collection of eighteenth-century types, most of them scoundrels, who run the social gamut from the scapegrace young gentleman and the rich route to the dregs of slum life. London at this time supported some of the worst slums in the world (and continued to do so until early in this century) and the author seems to have known them well. An example of the loose morals prevalent within the upper class is provided by the gentleman whom Moll meets in a gambling parlor. In his case alcohol breaks down an already weak character. His remorse over his "seduction" of Moll is really no more than fear of disease, and once he finds there is no danger from her he wishes to repeat the experience. The shopkeepers who try to catch Moll with their stolen goods, the innumerable apprentices, servants, and the heroine's accomplices in crime make up the fabric of English life which Defoe knows so well and describes so accurately. By the time we have finished *Moll Flanders* we have the feel of the age-the noises, sights and smells, the very texture of eighteenth-century London.

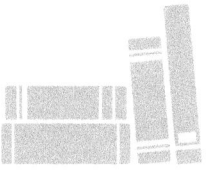

MOLL FLANDERS

CRITICAL COMMENTARY

THE ORIGIN OF THE NOVEL

Daniel Defoe has attracted a surprising and perhaps disproportionate amount of interest from the critics. The reason for this interest lies in the fact that Defoe was writing at the time when the English novel was just coming into being as a distinct literary form, or **genre**. Most writers on Defoe deny him the honor of being the first English novelist. They maintain that a novel, as well as being an extended prose narrative, must be a coherent story in which all the parts contribute to the total effect. It must also have a consistent moral point of view that motivates the events, and must be concerned largely with personal relationships. As Ian Watt has pointed out in his extremely useful book, *The Rise of the Novel*, to which this commentary will make frequent reference, what Defoe has created is not so much the prototype of the novel as his own personal **genre**, in which characters who have many of the traits of the author himself are pitted in a struggle against a generally hostile society. *Moll Flanders* simply does not fit the usual pattern of the novel. As we have seen, it lacks coherence (since it consists of a large number of more or less unrelated incidents), it is almost exclusively concerned with material things rather than with personal relationships, and the moral idea which the modern reader derives from it is exceedingly cynical and unintended by the author. Credit for the origination of the novel as we know it is usually given to Samuel Richardson, a younger contemporary of Defoe, whose *Pamela,* published in 1740, at least formally fits the requirements. In spite of these technical considerations we must continue, for convenience, to call Defoe's fictional works novels for lack of any better name.

SOURCES FOR DEFOE'S NEW GENRE

Professor Arthur W. Secord, in *Studies in the Narrative Method of Defoe,* presents a convenient summary of theories about the origin of Defoe's fiction. There are, in his view, four major possibilities. Defoe may be continuing the style of the picaresque novel, in the tradition of Cervantes' *Don Quixote,* the sixteenth-century Spanish Lazarillo de Tormes, and the contemporary *Gil Blas* by Rene LeSage. The hero of the picaresque novel is a rogue (in Spanish, picaro) whose diverse adventures form the substance of the book. A second possibility is that Defoe's spurious biographies grow naturally out of his journalistic writing, in which much of the material was also invented. Since much of his journalism was intended as propaganda rather than "straight" reporting, a small increase in the proportion of fictional matter would result in the creation of a work such as *Captain Singleton, Robinson Crusoe,* or *Moll Flanders.* Another possible explanation has its origin in the popularity of books which purported to be the biographies of actual criminals (supposedly written by the criminal himself before his execution, but actually the work of literary hacks). The criminal biographies are similar in many ways to Defoe's works, although the name of an actual criminal is used. The final suggestion is that Defoe's biographical "novels," which are intended to be **didactic** (that is, to teach a moral lesson), are the outgrowth of his more forthright books of moral teaching. The most notable of these is his Family Instructor, which is a kind of encyclopedia of domestic behavior. Secord eliminates the first of these possibilities by pointing out that the adventures of the picaresque hero were designed to provide the occasion for **satire** of the upper classes, and Defoe has no such intention. The other three suggestions: that Defoe's novels have their origin in journalism, rogue biography, and moral instruction, are all in part true, Secord feels. In his study, which is focused primarily on *Robinson Crusoe*, Professor Secord also points out Defoe's indebtedness for source material to the numerous current books of travel and exploration. These books undoubtedly contributed to the detailed description presented in *Moll Flanders* of life in the American colonies. Defoe traveled extensively all over England, but never visited America.

DEFOE'S CONTRIBUTION TO THE DEVELOPMENT OF THE NOVEL

Defoe's use of the concepts of "formal **realism**" and "economic individualism" are seen by Ian Watt as his contribution to the emerging novel form. The word "**realism**" has been the subject of much critical debate, but we can define it simply (with relation to Defoe) as an attempt by an individual to make clear his own view of reality. It is a style of writing which gains much of its effect from a scrupulous attention to detail and attempts to show life "as it really is." In Defoe's time this meant the depiction of the seamy side of life (not previously considered a proper subject for literature) and the rejection of artificial stylistic **conventions** which detract from this sense of reality. Watt uses the term "formal **realism**" to remind the reader that **realism** itself is a formal literary device, and thus artificial by its very nature. The writer's art must enter into any literary work, no matter how "realistic." The exact reproduction of an event in all its detail is an impossibility, and even if it were possible, it would not be literature. Any literary work must go through a process of selection, the business of sifting a mass of impressions for the essential ones, of emphasizing some and rejecting others, the process which is controlled by what we call the imagination. This sort of **realism** is quite new in Defoe's time. He is its first successful practitioner in England. The concept of "economic individualism," as Watt calls it, will be discussed later with reference to Moll herself.

LITERATURE AND THE ART OF LYING

Part of the effectiveness of Defoe's realistic technique arises from the fact that he goes to considerable lengths to convince us that this is an actual autobiography-that every word in the book is literally true. There are several reasons why he should do this. For one thing, the people for whom he wrote, the middle class and the upper segments of the lower class, would be more interested if they thought they were reading the life of a real person. Defoe is here carrying on the tradition of the rogue biography. But there is also a contemporary moral reason for the author to maintain the truth of what he writes. As Alan McKillop points out in his book, *The Early Masters of English Fiction*, the attitude of the eighteenth century (and of ages before that) to fiction was different from our own. This attitude is demonstrated by the remark of William Minto, one of Defoe's nineteenth-century biographers. Defoe, Minto said, was "a great, a truly great liar, perhaps the greatest that ever lived." Minto reflects the older attitude that all fiction is a kind of lying. After all, it is a description of something that never really happened, and thus an untruth. If this attitude were carried to its logical extreme, no fiction would ever be written. Those who defended the usefulness of invented stories maintained the distinction between literal and **didactic** truth; a piece of writing might not be literally true, but it might teach truth or correct moral action. This argument was exactly the one that Defoe used in defending *Moll Flanders*. Like the propagandist he was, he had two lines of defense. The story is true, he maintained, and even if it isn't true, it teaches the reader the penalty of immoral actions.

THE CHARACTER OF MOLL FLANDERS

Second only to Defoe's contribution to the birth of the novel, the attention of critics has been occupied by the character of his heroine. The modern critics and biographers of Defoe, with the historical approach characteristic of much modern literary scholarship, look to the facts of the author's life and the circumstances of his time for an explanation of this character. One of the most puzzling things about Moll is the divergence between her words and her actions. What she says is morally impeccable, but what she does is not so much immoral as amoral. Her acts do not seem to take morality into account at all. In view of this contradiction, some critics have wondered whether Defoe meant his readers to take the opposition between word and deed as his ironic comment on contemporary morality. Recent Defoe critics, including the two most comprehensive modern biographers, James Sutherland in his *Defoe,* and John Moore in his *Daniel Defoe, Citizen of the Modern World*, feel that Defoe was not being ironic. They maintain that the narrowness of his religious beliefs and those of his contemporaries prevented author and audience alike from seeing any contradiction at all. Self-righteousness has been described as characteristic of the Puritan point of view; they could see the faults of others with a clarity that blinded them to their own. This is exactly Moll's fault, and because Defoe seems unaware of it, we can assume that it is his blind spot as well. The phenomenon can be seen among Puritans nearer home in the witch-hunters of seventeenth-century Salem, Massachusetts, and in Nathaniel Hawthorne's *Scarlet Letter*.

CONFLICT IN DEFOE'S PERSONALITY

Other critics have attempted to explain the contradiction in Moll's personality on the basis on the author's life. The most recent exponent of the "conflict" school of thought, Brian Fitzgerald, in his *Daniel Defoe, A Study in Conflict*, sees two opposed forces in Defoe's nature, the Puritan and the bohemian. According to Fitzgerald, Defoe either consciously or unconsciously reproduced this opposition in the character of *Moll Flanders*. The same tendency to interpret Defoe's life in the light of his writings (not the other way around) can be seen in the somewhat romanticized biography of Paul Dottin, *The Life and Strange and Surprising Adventures of Daniel De Foe*. Modern critics who are more familiar with the details of Defoe's career (John Moore, in particular) are wary of such an interpretation. They are inclined to attribute the author's ability to portray a paradoxical figure like Moll to his journalistic skill and his observation and knowledge of all kinds of men. Maximillian Novak specifically rejects the "conflict" theory in his *Economics and the Fiction of Daniel Defoe*. He maintains that Moll's behavior demonstrates the effectiveness of Defoe's realistic technique. In *Moll Flanders*, according to Novak, we see the world through the eyes of a criminal, and thus the distinction between good and evil is deliberately blurred.

NATURAL LAW IN MOLL FLANDERS

An interesting interpretation of Moll's actions, with their violation of conventional morality, can be found in Maximillian Novak's *Defoe and the Nature of Man*. Novak points out that the concept of natural law was arousing great interest in Defoe's time. This law, which man finds to be inherent within himself, is more basic than and supersedes philosophy and Christian ethics. Defoe uses the concept of natural law when it is reduced to its essence: the one duty which every man has, and which overrides all others, is to survive. The author could see in his own life, and all around him, this law of self-preservation at work, and he uses it as the primary motivation of Moll's conduct. This interpretation of the heroine's behavior is closely related to Ian Watt's term, "economic individualism." Watt points out that the seventeenth century brought a change in social outlook, a change which caused people to be regarded as individuals, not collectively as members of organizations such as the Church, the guild or the manor. This individualism was particularly novel and important in the economic field; each person was an economic entity, and could prosper or starve as a result of his own efforts or lack of them. While this view may be extreme and unduly harsh as an interpretation of actual economic conditions in the seventeenth and eighteenth centuries, there can be no doubt that Moll sees her situation in just this way. As Watt points out, her actions are the result of her feeling that she is completely alone, her sense of alienation. Because she has no one to depend on economically but herself, most of her story is a search for security, either through marriage (the customary means for a woman at that time), or through accumulation of a fortune. The striking emphasis in *Moll Flanders* on things, tangible objects such as pieces of cloth or of gold, is a result of this quest for security.

THE SIMILARITY BETWEEN MOLL FLANDERS AND DEFOE

A number of modern critics, particularly Ian Watt and John Moore in his *Daniel Defoe, Citizen of the Modern World*, point out just how autobiographical *Moll Flanders* is. In her economic and religious attitudes, if not in her morality, Defoe has made Moll much like himself. Both the author and his heroine are ceaselessly on the lookout for a way to turn things to financial advantage; they are necessarily self-reliant, not especially introspective, and naturally gregarious. In smaller things the relationship also holds true. Defoe loved to travel, and we see Moll taking this same pleasure in movement, in looking at the variety of city and country life. But like the author, London is Moll's first love, her spiritual home. Later in the century the English author Samuel Johnson was to say, "A man who is tired of London is tired of life." The epigram sums up Defoe's attitude exactly. *Moll Flanders* is a product of the city, of city thinking and a city way of life, in much the same way that Restoration comedy is.

DEFOE AS A MODERN MAN

As the title of John Moore's book indicates, Defoe was a very modern man far more so than most of his contemporaries. His interest in financial projects, his rejection of tradition, both literary and philosophical, and his (comparative) lack of class-consciousness in a snobbish age make him nearly unique in the early eighteenth century. The gulf that yawned between Defoe, the journalist, tradesman and literary hack, and the "respectable" authors of the time is pointed out by John Ross in his *Swift and Defoe, A Study in Relationship*. The two most striking books of the first third of the century, Defoe's *Robinson Crusoe* and Jonathan Swift's *Gulliver's Travels*, are superficially very similar. Both describe the hero's travels to strange places and his adventures among outlandish peoples. But Swift was a member of the accepted literary circle, the university educated and classically-oriented adherents of the aristocracy, who wrote for social or ecclesiastical advancement, not for money. Defoe, on the other hand, was a bourgeois author who made a living from his books during the latter part of his life. Swift uses an obviously fictional story to make a subtle moral and philosophical point. Defoe proclaims his moral purpose like a revivalist, but puts in plenty of sensational and scandalous detail to please the masses. Ross sees *Gulliver's Travels* and *Moll Flanders* as symbols of the conflict between the old order and the new in literature.

FAULTS IN THE NOVEL

A number of critics, particularly those of an older generation, have concentrated on the flaws in *Moll Flanders*. There are plenty of faults to choose from. One of the first is that the book is not a novel at all in the generally accepted sense of the word. It belongs to a **genre** of its own, and of course Defoe made no claim that it was a novel. A more serious criticism is the lack of coherence in the story. As James Sutherland has pointed out in *Defoe,* it seems to consist of a number of **episodes** which are not related in any way. This view has been challenged by Terence Martin in "The Unity of Moll Flanders," an article in *Modern Language Quarterly* for 1961. He maintains that the novel is unified, at least as far as motivation and geography are concerned. He sees Moll's efforts as an attempt, in the second part of the story, to win back the security she has known as a wife in the first part. In middle age she revisits all the scenes of her early life as stages in this attempt; the geographical pattern of the novel is circular. While Martin certainly has some facts on the side of his interpretation, we are at liberty to wonder whether Defoe consciously organized the book in this way.

DEFOE'S STYLE

Important criticisms of Defoe's style can be found in Maximillian Novak's *Defoe and the Nature of Man* and Ian Watt's *The Rise of the Novel*. Novak points out that while the author is extremely good at realistic description, the mustering of concrete details which make street scenes and shop windows real to the reader, he is not nearly as skillful at describing individual reactions. Defoe is inclined to give a clinical picture of the emotion itself, not of the person undergoing the sensation. The writer's deficiency here helps to account for the apparent coldness of Moll herself. He simply could not portray effectively a person in the grip of deep feeling. At the same time Defoe's realistic skill is such that he convinces us that this coldness is part of Moll's character. We feel that she should be cold and calculating-the lack of deeply felt emotion does not disturb us. Other defects of Defoe style have already been discussed. There is his failure to connect the **episodes** of his story into a coherent pattern, and the apparent lack of any central point of view. One point for which Defoe's contemporaries criticized him, however, no longer bothers us. They were appalled at his vulgarity, at his inclusion of the sordid details of underworld life. In a little over two hundred years we have become a good deal harder to shock; today *Moll Flanders* makes fairly tame reading.

THE TREND OF DEFOE CRITICISM

Fashions in the discussion of Defoe's novels have followed a general trend in literary criticism. The older critics (and some modern ones) have tried to interpret the novels in the light of the facts of Defoe's own life, and have sometimes made his life seem very romantic to fit his novels. The biographies of William Minto and Paul Dottin, as well as the more recent one of Brian Fitzgerald, are examples of this kind of criticism. These writers tend to see the author as an isolated individual, uninfluenced by such things as public acclaim or lack of it, or the state of the market for literature. Modern criticism, with its more historical approach, tries to see the writer in the context of a detailed knowledge of the history, particularly the social and literary climate, of his time. This is the approach of John Moore, of James Sutherland (whose Background for Queen Anne is a fascinating study of life in the eighteenth century), and of Ian Watt. Watt's *Rise of the Novel*, for instance, devotes a good deal of space to an examination and appraisal of the growing reading public during Defoe's time. Such an approach is especially useful in the case of Defoe because he is so much the product of his age. As Sutherland points out, his life and his thinking were strongly and directly influenced by political and economic events. He was vitally concerned about writing a book which would interest the largest possible reading public, a book which would sell. Unlike "respectable" writers of the day, his livelihood depended on the popularity of his works. An example will illustrate the importance of the historical background. To understand why *Moll Flanders* is the kind of book it is, it is extremely useful to know that rogue biographies were tremendously popular in Defoe's time. The enthusiasm for criminal lives makes it unlikely that the author deliberately set out to invent a new **genre** in *Moll Flanders*. It is far more reasonable to think that he intended to take advantage of an already popular form, and in his gifted hands the biographical form was improved until it became a new **genre**. As we can see, Defoe provides one of the more rewarding demonstrations of the value of historical criticism.

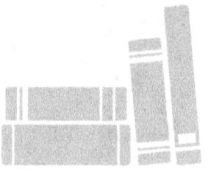

MOLL FLANDERS

ESSAY QUESTIONS AND ANSWERS

The questions and discussions provided here are intended to help the reader delve more deeply into *Moll Flanders*. Ideally they should make him think about the structure of the book as a whole, wonder about certain points that may have been taken for granted at first reading, and ask further questions of his own. These questions are general, and no attempt has been made to provide a definitive answer or say the last word in the case. Critics have been arguing about the same topics for generations.

Question: Why does Defoe make *Moll Flanders* realistic and how does he go about it?

Answer: No one would deny the fact that *Moll Flanders* is a piece of realistic fiction. Defoe, however, is so successful in this **genre** that we tend to forget that the realistic novel is in large part his own invention. There are comparatively few works of fiction before Defoe's time which attempt to pass themselves off to the audience as true, and in which such an effort is made to convince the readers of that fact.

There are, of course, good reasons for all this effort. There is the old belief, which can be traced back to the time of the Greeks, and was held especially strongly by the Puritans who made up a large segment of Defoe's audience, that any work of imagination is a kind of lying. Defoe tried to counter this objection by maintaining that his work was a true biography. He then hedged by saying that even if it wasn't true, it was morally beneficial. There is also the fact that Defoe's audience came from the middle and lower classes: tradesmen, servants, apprentices and the like. These were people whose approach to literature was unsophisticated. They liked what the same group of readers likes today-a fast-moving plot to hold the attention, not a complicated one diluted with sub-plots. This is precisely the audience which is now reading the James Bond thrillers. They like characters who are easy to understand, people with whom they can identify, and that means essentially people like themselves. But to hold the attention of these readers the commonplace characters in the book must do scandalous or bizarre or heroic things which the reader would never think of doing. Defoe's public had to be convinced, just as Ian Fleming's audience must be today (if only temporarily), that what they were reading was true.

Defoe achieves the effect of **realism** primarily by a concentration on concrete detail. The technique does not depend on a minute description of landscapes or buildings such as we get in the fiction of the Romantic period. It is rather an emphasis on the things in which his audience is interested-the London streets and their inhabitants, together with objects of value: cloth and clothing, plate (by which Defoe meant sterling silverware), rich food, and above all, money. Notice the amount of sheer enumeration in *Moll Flanders*. Moll is forever counting things, running them through her fingers, estimating their value. Although during the first part of the novel she is supposed to be a simple housewife, she already appears to be an expert on the cost of things, keeping detailed accounts and continuously aware of her own net worth. During Moll's career as a pickpocket and thief we are fascinated by her escapes. She seems to know every lane and alley of that rabbit-warren, eighteenth-century London, and we are whisked up one street and down another, around corners and into doorways, until we are as breathless as Moll herself.

Verisimilitude, the appearance of reality, is achieved in another way: by feigning ignorance, forgetfulness, or disclaiming knowledge. How often Moll says, "We stayed at an inn, I forget the name." This remark seems so natural that we accept it without thinking. It is quite understandable that someone should forget these details, and we are persuaded that Moll is a real person; at the same time we are convinced of the accuracy of what she does remember. Another factor in Defoe's realistic techniques has been called a fault by a number of observers, and on the strength of it some would deny him a place as a real novelist. This is the fact that he subordinates personal relationships, which many critics feel should be central to the novel. Though she claims to be very warm-hearted, even passionate, in her dealings with others, Moll is actually brusque; she never lets them interfere with her own interests. But the attitude of every man for himself was typical of the class to which the novel appealed. To this new mercantile middle class there were few loyalties beyond the family, and Moll has no family. We come to feel, as we read the book, that attention to things rather than people is not a flaw in Defoe's technique, but simply typical of Moll herself, a natural outgrowth of her personality.

Another effect which could be attributed to faulty writing becomes instead an adjunct of **realism**. This effect is the disjointed and episodic nature of the story. When Moll tells an **episode**, even a very fast-moving and exciting one, she constantly interrupts herself to make unnecessary or misplaced generalizations, she tells part of the tale in a tone of reminiscence and part as if the action is actually going on, and she is continually changing the subject. Yet instead of saying, "What an awkward writer Defoe is." we say, "Isn't that just like a woman?" Defoe has convinced us of the reality of Moll herself, and everything else flows naturally from that assumption. In this respect, the author is a supremely successful writer of fiction.

Question: In what ways is *Moll Flanders* unlike a contemporary novel?

Answer: Since Defoe appears among the very first writers of novels, we should not expect his work to conform in all respects to our conception of this form. The modern novel (theoretically at least) has a unified plot, it is concerned with the inner workings, the personalities, of its characters, and deals primarily with the interactions of these characters. The basic premise of the modern novel, reduced to the lowest common denominator, is that we are interested in reading about the lives of other people.

The literature of the early eighteenth century is based on an entirely different premise. To the people of Defoe's age, any kind of writing was primarily for instruction; it had to inculcate a moral truth and entertainment was a secondary and quite subsidiary goal. Defoe, then, had to start out with the idea that Moll's life must teach a lesson. That is why Moll has to tell her story at the end of her life, when she is looking back with regret on her evil career. This moral tone seems unfamiliar and forced to us today, but to Defoe's readers it was a necessary and even indispensable part of literature.

Defoe's novel is also concerned with things, with the concrete, the tangible, rather than with personal relationships. We still find this kind of novel current today, but it is not considered the most desirable or most "literary" kind. Adventure and particularly detective stories, which can be classed as novels if we use the term broadly, and especially science fiction with its gadgets, are examples of the same sort of technique. Another part of the appeal of *Moll Flanders* is the same as that of books of travel; it tells of far-off places, in this case of the American colonies.

Moll Flanders differs, at least from the ideal modern novel, because it is episodic; the incidents are not connected carefully enough to make a unified story. Moll simply proceeds from one adventure to another, and the incidents are not part of any larger structure. This lack of organization is particularly evident in the second part of the book, where the series of robberies fails to build up to a **climax**. The only suspense is provided by Moll's own comments about how she is going from bad to worse.

In spite of these differences between the modern novel and *Moll Flanders*, there are a good many similarities, and these are due in large part to something which is not a matter of time or place, namely, creative skill in writing. As a clever writer, Defoe is well aware of the usefulness of repetition; Moll's repeated statements and encounters with the same people for a second or third time give a reader the pleasure of familiarity. The author's talent for description is also something that he has in common with the better modern novelists. A good many novels of the nineteenth century, and some of those of our own time, have been given to florid and detailed accounts of places. Defoe does very little of this landscape painting; the scenes through which his characters pass are merely suggested by one or two significant details. Moll attempts to steal a lady's watch, "... in a crowd, at a meeting-house, ..." From this small hint we can reconstruct the jostling, the pressure of bodies against each other, the whole atmosphere of the place. In his effective building on a single detail Defoe's technique is like that of the nineteenth-century French writer Marcel Proust and the contemporary Albert Camus.

For all its faults and its strangeness, the modern reader recognizes *Moll Flanders* as a successful piece of fiction. It is not organized like a modern novel, and perhaps not even like a work of art. Still it attracts us, for it has both the confusion and the predictability of life.

Question: Defoe has been called a modern man and one of the earliest modern authors. Can evidence for this statement be found in *Moll Flanders*?

Answer: To avoid confusion, let us define a "modern" man as one whom we recognize as belonging to our time, one whose actions and motivations we can understand in our own terms. We have already said repeatedly that Defoe is a realistic author. The very fact that he is interested in realism marks him as modern at the beginning of the eighteenth century. Earlier writers, as far back as English prose and poetry go, and beyond that to the classical origins of literature, were not interested in the originality of their story. A new plot was considered quite unnecessary, as a study of Chaucer's sources, or Shakespeare's, will show. What writers before Defoe's time did consider necessary was the shaping of the already familiar plot in an artistic way in accordance with the accepted literary **conventions** of the time. But Defoe was not conventional in his approach to writing. He was not a member of the London literary cliques as Joseph Addison, Richard Steele and Jonathan Swift were; he did not even belong to the same social class. His motivation for writing was also quite different.

He was writing for money, rather desperately, as a way of making a living and redeeming himself from bankruptcy. He did not care for the acclaim of the intellectuals but for cash on the barrelhead. In this he is conspicuously modern, for authorship was to become, with increasing momentum after Defoe's time, a profession for the literate but needy rather than a pastime for the leisured classes.

In looking at literature as a profession Defoe had to be concerned with the widest possible audience, and this was not the most sophisticated or even the most literate one. His readers were concerned not with the polishing of a familiar story but with the new and sensational, and that is exactly what Defoe gave them. His realistic technique is part of his attempt to convince his readers that what they are seeing is real, part of the daily life they are interested in, and not "mere" fiction.

Defoe's own life can be shown to have been modern rather than traditional. He was an entrepreneur, making use of capital to finance a number of ventures rather than working at one trade all his life in the accepted bourgeois pattern. And while the point is a debatable one, his morality also seems modern. His standards were relative, shaped to fit the situation, rather than bound by absolute rules. This pattern of behavior is made very clear by Moll's actions. Whenever she is forced to choose between Christian morality and her own advantage, she voices the very modern doctrine that everyone has to look after himself, and takes the course more profitable for her. In doing this she pleads the law of self-preservation (part of the law of nature according to the thinking of Defoe's time) and makes it her excuse for the violation of conventional standards. While the law of self-preservation was certainly no novelty in the eighteenth century, its use as a motive in a work of literature is new.

Even the mechanics of Defoe's writing belong to the modern age rather than to the past. Unlike his self-consciously "literary" predecessors, who felt the need to write slowly and make corrections as they went along, our author was enormously prolific. In the year *Moll Flanders* was written he turned out 1500 printed pages. This breakneck speed shows itself in inconsistencies within the novels and in repetitions of the same formulas, both of plot and of expression. It was a standing joke among his fellow writers that he never revised anything unless he was paid extra by the publisher to do so. Though the statement may seem cynical, the emphasis on quantity rather than quality in writing is a modern trait.

Moll Flanders can be seen as part of the new trend in fiction in its emphasis on concrete detail, on travel, on the life of the streets and of the lower and middle classes, on the awareness that Britain was, as it was to be called in the next century, "a nation of shopkeepers." All this is exactly what we should expect from the lucid, bourgeois and very commonplace mind of Defoe. Moll is like Defoe himself; the book is autobiographical because the man was a clever journalist who knew the value of talking about something he was familiar with. But Defoe also makes Moll like himself because he is provincial. Clever though he is, he cannot really see into the minds of others, but views them as variations on his own mind. The point of view of *Moll Flanders* is insular (look at Jemmie's reluctance to leave England even though his life is at stake) and here too Defoe is ahead of his time. From the cosmopolitan and relatively "international" attitude of the Augustan Age, England was to retreat in the next century into an insularity which it had not known since the Middle Ages.

Defoe makes use of and helps to invent a new direction in literature and even gives us a preview of much of the social thinking in the next century. *Moll Flanders* establishes, as clearly as any of his novels, the title which John Moore gives him, "Citizen of the Modern World."

Question: Is Moll Flanders a sympathetic character?

Answer: Superficially Moll seems to be a hard woman. She is single-mindedly devoted to her own interests and always on the lookout for something that she may turn to her advantage. At the same time her mentality is so limited (or Defoe's art in portraying her is so inadequate) that we have difficulty in identifying with her. Throughout the book she remains rather two-dimensional.

As we advance through the book, however, we find ourselves enjoying Moll more and more. She is so forthright, so direct. Her deceit, for she considers herself full of wiles, is that of a child who thinks it has done no wrong if it does not tell a direct lie. Look, as an example, at the care she takes to avoid telling her suitors that she has a fortune, though she uses every trick to give the impression of wealth. Such methods would only fool someone as greedy, as childish and as unperceptive as herself. Her crimes are often the result of actual need, though not so often as she would have us believe. In spite of her supposed repentance, she always has an excuse ready after the deed, and the excuses are as transparent as the deceit.

As a result we both laugh at and like Moll for her directness and childishness. But in the portrait as Defoe gives it there is room for admiration too. No matter what Moll's shortcomings on the moral plane, she has no lack of courage. To understand the extent of Moll's valor we have to be aware of the social position of women early in the eighteenth century. When Moll says how utterly adrift she is after the death of her first husband, she is not exaggerating her position. A married woman had no property rights, either in land or money, and an unmarried or widowed woman was prey for any acquisitive male. There was no way for a single woman to earn a living except by needlework, which would hardly provide a subsistence, or by selling her favors, as Defoe points out so fully in Roxana. Moll faces poverty and abandonment not once but a number of times during the novel, but each time her native wit pluckily finds a way out of the problem. She is ready to try anything: marriage, theft, farming in Ireland or America, genteel prostitution, any course that will enable her to survive. She even adapts quickly enough to the horrors of Newgate Prison. Moll has the grit of the English lower classes as Defoe saw them, the unreflective bulldog determination which may go down fighting but which will never stop fighting for an instant. In spite of the disasters of her career, one of the things that attracts us to Moll is the glamor of success. She has triumphed over adversity, and one level of her story has the same appeal as the works of Horatio Alger. Where an aristocrat would surrender, pine and die or commit suicide, Moll keeps plugging along and ends up contended, rich, and (because of her last-minute repentances) in a fair way of going to heaven.

Question: How is **irony** used in *Moll Flanders*?

Answer: **Irony** helps to provide a good deal of the dramatic effect in *Moll Flanders*. To discuss it accurately, however, we must distinguish between two kinds, conscious and unconscious **irony**. Conscious irony is the use of words out of their natural context or meaning for sarcastic or derisive effect. This kind of **irony** is used only occasionally and mildly by Defoe. But unconscious **irony**, what we can call the irony of fate - the fact that incidents or circumstances have results which we could not possibly foresee, is omnipresent.

Moll uses conscious **irony** to comment on the behavior of those she observes, usually to point out that their actions are not in accordance with their own statements or with the role they are trying to assume. Sometimes it is difficult to tell if Moll is using mild **irony** or is simply looking at the world without illusions, in her usual clear-sighted way. For instance she tells how, at the age of ten, the ladies of Colchester would give her nurse clothes or money for the little girl. The nurse used these to dress her prettily, "... and would always tell the ladies this or that was bought with their money; and this made them oftentimes give me more ..." While Moll herself seems almost unconscious of the fact, the remark is a cutting commentary on those who insist upon seeing the tangible results of their charity.

As opposed to the rather infrequent use of conscious **irony**, Defoe's use of the **irony** of fate is structural; it provides one of the main **themes** of the novel. There is the ironic disparity, for instance, between the kind of life that Moll expects and works for, and the kind she is forced to live. Even as a little girl respectability and security are her main goals; she wants to be a "gentlewoman." Yet her hopes are continually being shattered by forces absolutely beyond her control. She looks for safety in marriage, which was the only sensible place for a woman to look in the eighteenth century. But all five of her husbands turn out to be either scoundrels or else they die within a few years of marriage. Moll tries again and again, but fate is too strong for her. It is terribly ironic that when she has risked the dangerous voyage and is finally settled in America with the prospect of future safety and even prosperity, her husband should turn out to be also her half-brother.

The ending of the book provides this same kind of **irony** in reverse. Throughout her criminal career what Moll fears most is detection, conviction, and being committed to Newgate Prison.

Yet this event, when it finally happens, is not only less terrifying than she expected (she adapts to Newgate quickly), but prison is a gateway to a new and finally successful life in the Colonies. In jail she is reunited with the husband she loves most, and she not only rescues herself but is the means of rescuing him.

Irony, then, provides a great deal of the interest, and perhaps even accounts for our emotional involvement with Moll's fate. We only identify with Moll to a limited extent, but our attention is held as we wonder what bizarre course her life will take next. One of the morals that Defoe did not intend us to draw from his novel is nevertheless very clear; life is utterly unpredictable.

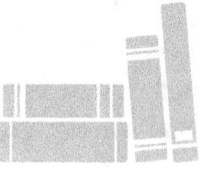

MOLL FLANDERS

GLOSSARY OF TERMS

BAILIFF

In Defoe's time, an officer of the law who served warrants, made arrests and took charge of prisoners.

CLOWN

Defoe means by this word a country fellow, a simple peasant, not the circus variety of clown.

COMPOSITION (FOR DEBT)

To make a composition for debt in bankruptcy is to agree to pay one's creditors a percentage of what they are owed, such as twenty-five cents in the dollar.

CONSTABLE

Constables at this time were not full-time policemen, but part-time ones who usually held another job as well. They generally did not patrol an area but were summoned to restore order or take a prisoner to the magistrate.

DRAPER (USUALLY, LINEN-DRAPER)

A dealer in cloth and linens, as well as some finished goods.

FOWLING-PIECE

A light gun, usually smooth-bored, used for shooting birds (wild fowl).

GUINEA

An English monetary unit, worth twenty-one shillings, or one pound and one shilling. Gold guineas were struck during Defoe's time, supposedly of gold from the African country of Guinea. Though the coins have not been minted since 1813, the unit is still used in England, especially in quoting large prices.

HOLLAND

A fairly light and finely-woven cloth of linen (or more rarely in Defoe's day, cotton).

JADE

A bad-tempered or disreputable woman; also a vicious or worn-out horse, although Defoe does not use the word in this latter sense.

JOINTURE

An estate or sum of money given by the husband to the wife at marriage for her exclusive use.

LIVERY

The uniform in which wealthy people, especially the nobility, dressed their servants.

MERCER

A dealer in textiles. In the eighteenth century the term usually referred to someone who was at least partially a wholesaler.

PLATE

Cups, serving pieces, candlesticks, etc. made out of sterling silver. The collection of plate usually constituted a family's most valuable movable possession. Plate in this sense has nothing to do with plated ware as we know it; the technique of electroplating was not invented until the nineteenth century.

POSTILLION

A servant, usually a boy, who rides one of the horses that pulls the coach. Like the footman, the postillion was not strictly necessary, and thus having one became a status symbol.

SPONGING-HOUSE

A place where people arrested for debt are kept for a day to give them a chance to arrange their affairs with their creditors.

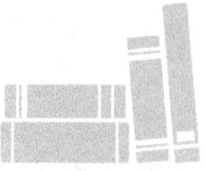

BIBLIOGRAPHY

The following books and articles contain biographical information on Defoe and critical material on his novels. Most general criticism of Defoe's works contains some discussion of *Moll Flanders*. The books starred are available in paperback.

Defoe, *Daniel Letters*. Edited by George H. Healey. Oxford: Clarendon Press, 1955. Defoe's correspondence, much of it confidential reports to Robert Harley, is essential for an understanding of his political career.

Defoe, Daniel. *Moll Flanders*. New York: Random House, 1950. (Modern Library Edition). Mark Schorer's "Introduction" to the Modern Library Edition provides an excellent summary of criticism and background material.

Dobree, Bonamy. "Some Aspects of Defoe's *Prose*" in *Pope and His Contemporaries*, Essays Presented to George Sherburn. Edited by Clifford and Landa. Oxford: Clarendon Press, 1949. Dobree, an extremely well-known critic, discusses Defoe's achievement with particular reference to the use of irony in *Moll Flanders*.

Dottin, Paul. *The Life and Strange and Surprising Adventures of Daniel De Foe*. Translated from the French by Louise Ragan. New York: The Macaulay Co., 1929. Dottin's biography of Defoe is emotional and somewhat eccentric, but interesting.

Fitzgerald, Brian. *Daniel Defoe: A Study in Conflict.* Chicago: Henry Regnery and Co., 1955. Fitzgerald interprets Defoe's life as a conflict between the Puritan and the bohemian sides of his nature. This interpretation is useful, but not all modern critics agree with it.

Mckillop, Alan D. *The Early Masters of English Fiction.* Lawrence: University of Kansas Press, 1956. Defoe is among the early novelists discussed in this up-to-date work on the origins of the novel.

Martin, Terrence. "The Unity of *Moll Flanders*," *Modern Language Quarterly*, Volume XXII, 1961, pp. 115–124. Martin maintains that motivation and geography provide a unity which is lacking in *Moll Flanders* at first glance.

Minto, William. *Daniel Defoe, London, 1879.* This early biography of Defoe is still considered authoritative by the critics.

Moore, John Robert. *Daniel Defoe: Citizen of the Modern World.* Chicago: University of Chicago Press, 1958. Moore's book is the most detailed modern study of Defoe's life.

Novak, Maximillian E. *Defoe and the Nature of Man.* London: Oxford University Press, 1963. A study of Defoe's prose in the light of eighteenth-century philosophy, Novak's book is specialized but provocative.

Novak, Maximillian E. *Economics and the Fiction of Daniel Defoe.* University of California English Studies, No. 24. Berkeley: University of California Press, 1962. Novak rejects the "conflict" interpretation of Defoe's life and explains the relationship between Defoe as novelist and as propagandist.

Ross, John F. *Swift and Defoe: A Study in Relationship.* Berkeley: University of California Press, 1941. The contrast between Swift, the would-be aristocrat who wrote for promotion, and Defoe, the middle-class merchant who wrote for money, illustrates the changing position of the writer in eighteenth century society.

Secord, Arthur W. *Studies in the Narrative Method of Defoe*. New York: Russell and Russell, Inc., 1963. Secord's book is primarily on Defoe's use of source material in *Robinson Crusoe* and two other novels (not *Moll Flanders*), but his summary of Defoe criticism and bibliography are very useful.

Stephen, Leslie. "Defoe's Novels," in *Hours in a Library*. London, 1899. Sir Leslie presents the attitudes toward Defoe, many of them still very sound, of an older generation of critics.

Sutherland, James. *Defoe*. London: Methuen and Co., 1950. Better than any other modern writer Sutherland gives us the background of the times and shows us Defoe's place in eighteenth century life.

Tillyard, E. M. W. *The **Epic** Strain in the English Novel*. Fair Lawn, N.J.: Essential Books, Inc., 1958. Tillyard's book includes an interesting discussion of Defoe's novels as part of the **epic** tradition.

Watson, Frances. *Daniel Defoe*. (*Men and Books Series*.) New York: Longman's Green and Co., 1952. While it provides no new material, Watson's book is a competent standard biography and critical analysis of Defoe.

Watt, Ian. *The Rise of the Novel: Studies in Defoe, Richardson, and Fielding*: Berkeley: University of California Press, 1962. Watt's chapter on *Moll Flanders* is the single most important critical analysis of the book. His brilliant insights are indispensable for any serious student.

www.ingramcontent.com/pod-product-compliance
Lightning Source LLC
LaVergne TN
LVHW011710060526
838200LV00051B/2842